Fox and Geese and Fences

Fox and Geese and Fences

A Collection
of Traditional Maine Mittens

by Robin Hansen

Down East Books, Camden, Maine

For Aunt Bert and
Nora Johnson

Copyright © 1983 by Robin Hansen
ISBN 0-89272-162-6
Library of Congress Catalog Card Number 82-74083
Text design by Kate Titus
Cover design by Bonnie Bishop
Composition by Roxmont Graphics
Printed in the United States of America

10 9 8 7 6 5 4 3 2

Down East Books, Camden, Maine

Contents

Preface

Nowadays much winter clothing, including our mittens and caps, down vests and jackets, is made in southern countries — Haiti, Taiwan, even Hong Kong — by people who have never seen snow or had to deal with extreme cold. I've often wondered what they think about as they sit perspiring in a factory, stitching snowsuits for little children in Maine or Alaska. Are the snowsuits tried on by little brown boys and girls over their shorts and T-shirts? Are rubber boots slid on over bare feet?

Strangely enough, most of these winter clothes are fine, but the mittens are usually just silly, knit from brightly colored synthetic yarns, and so thin that one can see skin through the stitches. Some are covered with plastic that keeps out the wet but not the cold. The people who made them clearly didn't understand winter, and so, for mittens, northern peoples must rely on their own traditions and products.

In Maine, mittens are knit for density and for thickness with good mobility. Few dragon puppets or Santa Claus mittens are found here; you find instead just a good understanding of wool and its properties. Mittens are knit tightly with a single strand of wool yarn, or knit with special stitches that increase the thickness, or knit very large and shrunk by methods non-Mainers find incredible. Some Maine mittens are meant to be worn wet, soaked in salt water and wrung out before each wearing. Inland in Maine, mittens are knit with two strands of yarn in close all-over patterns reminiscent of the palm of a Norwegian mitten. This gives a double layer of wool with a lightness and mobility impossible with two layers of mittens or in a true double-knit mitten — that is, a mitten within a mitten, joined at the cuff.

Another traditional Maine mitten is knit with bits of combed fleece tucked into the knit, creating a fluffy lining that changes to a thick, woolly mat with use.

All these mittens are worn and loved by everyone in Maine who can get hold of them — but that is in fact the problem. There have been no written patterns, and the art is no longer passed from mother to daughter. Most women who knit these specialized, warm mittens are in their seventies.

This book is written to change this, to bring an old warm tradition into the reach of young women and men who prefer to knit from a pattern, or who have no grandmother or great aunt to teach them directly.

The patterns have been collected from all corners of Maine. I have also stretched a hand across into the Canadian Maritimes for some information, as these provinces share much of this tradition with Maine.

The only patterns presented here are those which traditionally are found in Maine, although some also occur in Canada. In some cases, I have added patterns for matching caps, although they are not at all part of the tradition.

Some of the patterns are said to be two hundred years old, but generally their origins are lost. Similar mittens are knit in the Hebrides and in parts of Sweden, but apparently only in cold countries with Northern British and Scandinavian-rooted populations.

Good knitting and warm hands to you!

General Instructions

The most general instructions I can give you are to ask you to **read the instructions**. These are old patterns that have been around for generations, and all the different ways of doing things here have a reason behind them. If you don't do it right, you'll probably do it wrong, waste your own time and materials, and wonder what happened. So do **read** and study the photos carefully.

There are many odd ways of doing things in these patterns that usually only passed along from one person to another, in person. To simulate that immediacy, in case your grandma can't show you, we've made several photo-series for some of the harder-to-explain ideas. Others, like several odd ways of increasing, you will have to piece together by reading about them.

Materials: Most of the mittens and caps here are made with worsted weight yarns. Those used here are Bartlettyarns 2-ply Homespun, Brunswick Germantown (a 4-ply worsted), and Briggs and Little's 2-ply worsted from Canada (sold by Candide in the United States). All these yarns are very similar in the thickness of the strand. When knitting a mitten which is supposed to have ridges, be sure the yarn that's supposed to form the ridge is as thick as the color for the background. The yarn on top can be thicker, but not thinner, or there will be no obvious ridges.

In the Baby Foxes and Goslings section, the baby mittens are knit with standard fingering weight yarn, and the small children's with standard sport weight yarn.

The Fishermen's Wet Mittens and the Incredible Checkerboard Mittens are knit with 3-ply fisherman yarn from Bartlettyarns, Harmony, Maine. If this is not available locally, it can be approximated. It's a naturally oily yarn about half again as thick as worsted yarn. Perhaps Irish fisherman yarn, the kind used for Aran sweaters, could be doubled. Experiment.

On the subject of wool versus synthetics: In the first snowfall last winter, our children burst out of the house in whatever winter clothes they could find — last year's jackets, unmatched boot socks and mittens, and caps that were too big or too small.

About ten minutes later, my seven-year-old was back inside, in tears. "My hand is so cold!" he wept, shaking it splashily.

On that hand he was wearing a mitten made of a synthetic yarn. It was soaked like a wet mop, it was heavy, and it was freezing cold.

The other hand, which emerged from its mitten rosy and steamy warm (I'm not exaggerating), was wearing a wool double-knit mitten, like the ones you'll find in this book. It was covered with caked-on wet snow. But it was dry inside.

Some Maine women tell me wool is harsh to knit with. If you think so, choose a softer wool. Commercial worsteds like Brunswick Germantown are not harsh.

Other Maine women who love synthetics tell me you can throw the synthetic mittens in the washer, launder them, then throw them in the dryer. I haven't yet figured out why this should be an important feature for anything but a baby mitten. Winter is usually over before mittens get washed in our house.

Of course, wool does shrink. Some women overcome this problem by washing the yarn in the skein in hot water before knitting it. Others knit the mitten slightly larger than the hand, to be shrunk informally on the radiator. Fishermen's Wet Mittens, also of wool, are knit much larger, then boiled and soaked in salt water. These shrink a lot.

Wool insulates when wet. Acrylic doesn't.

Equipment: Needle sizes given are American standard sizes, but in case you're reading this book in Oslo or Toronto, here are the approximate metric and Canadian equivalents.

American	Canadian	Metric
0	14	2
1	13	2.5
2	11	3
3	10	3
4	9	3.5
5	8	4
6	7	4.5

Knitting needle conversions are always approximate, but most yarn stores — even yarn departments in big discount stores — will usually let you knit a 2-inch square to check your tension, if you bring your own yarn. If they don't, try elsewhere.

Gauge: Please don't ever knit anything without making a test gauge to check your tension. Most people knit at about the same tension (or tightness) on a given size knitting needle, but maybe the pattern designer doesn't. Maybe in a jacquard (double-knit) you won't.

The one time you don't make a test gauge may be the one time the designer had a knit tight enough to repel pygmy blowgun darts, or loose enough to be used as gill nets for tuna. You never know until you make a test gauge.

Do this by casting on about 15 stitches on the same size needles and with the same yarn you plan to use for your project. Knit back and forth with stockinette stitch in the pattern you plan to use.

If your flat knitting differs from your knitting-in-the-round, cast on about 21 stitches on 3 double-pointed needles — 7 to a needle — and knit around in the pattern you'll use.

Knit about 2 inches. Then, push and pull the piece a little, flatten it out, and measure it across the stitches in the middle where there's no pull from either edge, the needles, or casting on. Count how many stitches are within one inch. Count half-stitches too. If you're in doubt, count across two inches and divide by two.

If there is a half-stitch too many within your inch, try the next American-size larger needles. For a half-stitch too few, go to the next size smaller. If you're shy a whole stitch, go down two sizes, and so forth.

Sizes: The sizes are pretty clearly stated in the instructions. What isn't stated is that large children wear small adult-size mittens and caps. And small men's hands can fit quite comfortably in women's medium-size mittens.

Women's medium is the same length as men's medium, but the men's size is wider.

Men's large is enormous. If I had followed the large size on a locally available Maine pattern, it would have been even more enormous, but I couldn't find anyone with a hand big enough to fit it, so I figured their sizing might be excessively large.

Abbreviations have been kept to the bare minimum to make the instructions more readable.

Any that aren't included below are explained in the text of the instructions where they are used.

dec	decrease
dk	dark
dp	double-pointed, as in dp knitting needles
inc	increase
k	knit
lt	light
no.	number, as in no. 3 knitting needles
p	purl
st,sts	stitch, stitches

Part One

Shrinking Mittens

Fishermen's Wet Mittens

Time was, when a man went out in his boat in winter, he took his mittens off a nail on the boat, dipped them in the warm water from the engine, wrung them out good, and put them on wet. Then he began hauling traps or working with bait.

His hands stayed warm in the wet wool mittens even working with wet traps dragged out of a frigid Casco Bay. When he peeled the mittens off later, his hands were so warm they steamed in the cold air. Then he hung them up again by little loops in their cuffs and went ashore.

The warm wool mittens had an amazing insulating quality — but only when wet, the fishermen say. They may have been knit by his wife, or he may have bought them — handknit — from the same store that sold him his trap stock, boots, netting shuttles and other gear. Wherever he got them, they were big, maybe a third bigger than his hand when new.

He took them home and boiled them or soaked them in hot water, and they shrank. The wool became thicker, the stitches tighter than can be knit. And as he wore them, wetting them in salt water each time, they shrank even more, became more matted, until they were molded to his hands and quite stiff when dry.

Fishermen wore mittens like these in Maine and Nova Scotia for hundreds of years. Some still do, when they can get them. In Newfoundland, they are still used, year-round.

In many fishing communities, the art of knitting fishermen's mittens was lost after the introduction of the insulated glove. Even those women who want to knit them for their husbands can't do so because there are no mittens left to measure, and no women left who know how to make them.

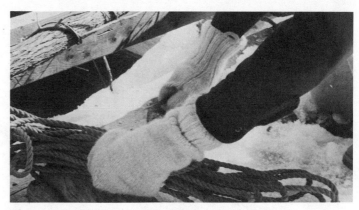

This was the case on Chebeague Island until a few years ago. Minnie Doughty, the one woman who had maintained the skill, had died, taking her knowledge with her.

Like many other coastal women, Mrs. Doughty had a difficult life and lost several of her six sons to the sea. In her lifetime she had knitted a great many pairs of fisherman mittens — so many, that when she died, the single remaining new pair was treasured as a keepsake by her daughters.

One of the expert knitters of the Chebeague Island Methodist Church Ladies Aid, Elizabeth Bergh, took these mittens, counted stitches, measured, found a loose end to determine the thickness of the yarn, and put together instructions for fishermen's mittens. These follow.

It can't be stressed enough that this pattern makes a huge mitten, which must be shrunk in hot salt water and dried, for example, on a radiator, at least once to be at all usable. The mitten is designed to be used wet, in salt water, by fishermen. The salt and the repeated soaking continue the shrinking process. Don't be disappointed if they don't shrink to size the first time!

Chebeague Island Fishermen's Wet Mittens

Materials: 4 ounces Bartlettyarns 3-ply fisherman yarn, or other heavy fisherman wool with lanolin. The mittens are traditionally cream-colored.

Equipment: 1 set no. 4 dp needles, or size needed for correct gauge. 1 medium crochet hook. 1 yarn needle.

Gauge: 5 sts = 1 inch.

Sizes: Men's large.

Cuff: On no. 4 dp needles, cast on 12, 15, and 15 sts (total 42 on 3 needles). K 2, p 1 until wristband measures 4 inches.

Then, first round: Place last p st on first needle. P 1, k 2, p 1. K rest of round, increasing 2 sts on each needle for a total of 48 sts.

Second round: Start thumb gore: p 1, inc 1 st in each of next 2 sts, p 1. K around, and k rounds 3, 4, and 5, maintaining the 2 p sts as markers.

Sixth round: P 1, inc in next stitch, k 2, inc in next st, p 1 (8 sts, including 2 p). K around. K 3 more rounds.

Continue to inc this way every fourth row until you have 14 sts for the thumb gore, including the 2 p sts. Knit 3 more rounds and place the 14 sts on a string.

Cast on 10 sts to bridge the gap and divide the sts, 18 to a needle (54 sts). K up 4 inches for the hand.

Dec: K 2 together, k 7, repeat to end of round.
K 2 rounds.
K 2 together, k 6, repeat to end of round.
K 2 rounds.
K 2 together, k 5, repeat to end of round.
K 2 rounds.
K 2 together, k 4, repeat to end of round.
K 1 round.
K 2 together all the way around and pull end through remaining sts.

Darn the end back and forth through the tip of the mitten, concealing the sts in the knit.

Thumb: Pick up from thumb gore 7 sts on 2 needles and 1 st from each side of the hole, for 8 sts on each needle. Pick up the 10 sts from the hand side on the third needle. Total 26 sts. K 2 rounds.

Next round, dec 1 st on both ends of third needle (now 8 sts on each needle.) K 2 inches.

Next round, dec: k 2 together, k 2, and repeat around. K 1 round. Next round: k 2 together, k 1, and repeat around. Pull end through remaining sts and darn through tip of thumb, concealing sts in the knit.

Crochet a loop at edge of cuff for hanging to dry. Use the tail left from casting on if possible. Minnie Doughty also buttonhole-stitched the loop for extra strength.

Children's Wet Mittens

To knit a mitten for a child who spends some time on a boat on the ocean, choose a pattern for worsted weight yarn and knit a mitten at least two sizes too large. The mitten will lose about one-quarter of its length but less in width. Follow the same instructions for shrinking, and don't forget the loop on the cuff!

Fleece-stuffed Mittens and Cap

Fleece-stuffed Mittens come from northern New-foundland and Labrador, but I have included them here because they belong to the same tradition as Maine Fishermen's Wet Mittens. They are often knit large and shrunk to size, and they appear to be made according to the same set of instructions except that a twist of unspun fleece is knit into every sixth stitch every sixth round.

The ends of the bits of fleece, fluffing to the inside, are thick and woolly, and mat into a continuous lining with wear, imitating the lining formed by fur on the inside of skin mittens.

They are beautiful mittens. Like Fishermen's Wet Mittens, they are knit of oiled natural yarn in natural colors. In dark brown and white fleece, they seem to show large flakes of snow falling softly against the night.

The pattern is no newcomer in Canada. Hazel McNeill, of Belleville, Ontario, wrote me that her mother and grandmother knit these mittens for their men, who used them both as a general outdoor mitten for dogsled travel and as a wet mitten for hauling nets in winter. She dates the pattern tentatively to the early 1800s.

In the areas where these mittens are used, icebergs still float in the ocean in August, and fishermen use a light wet mitten through the summer. Stuffed mittens seem like a logical extension of the wet-mitten concept.

In *Them Days*, an interview magazine about Labrador's past, stuffed or "drummed mitts" are referred to as children's mittens.

Fleece-stuffed Mittens have only a tenuous place in Maine folk knitting. I have only heard of one Maine woman who knits them; I have never met her or learned her name, and she was unwilling to discuss the mittens with my informant (Pat Zamore) other than to say that they have come down in her family.

Since I first learned of stuffed mittens, however, I've found that Maine people seem to like them and like to knit them. Perhaps they are spreading via traditional folk channels into Maine from the northern Maritime Provinces. So — a Maine folk mitten of the future, caught in passage.

Like other mittens in this book, this mitten uses techniques you may find nowhere else in the world. Read all the instructions carefully and study the pictures. Stuffed mittens aren't difficult to knit once you've made the first pair — a little tedious perhaps, but not difficult.

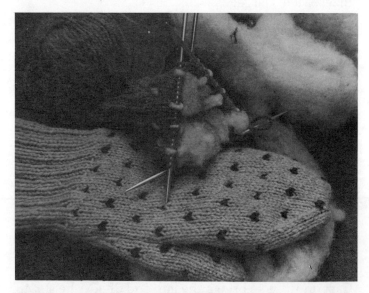

Fleece-stuffed Mittens have twisted bits of carded but unspun wool knitted into the fabric in a pattern. The ends of the bits of fleece, fluffing to the inside, form a warm, matted lining with use.

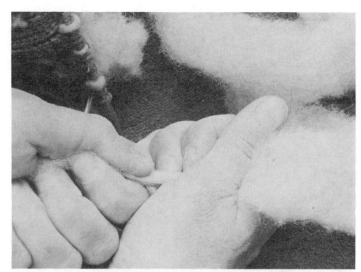

1 – Pull off a 5-inch length of 1-inch roving.

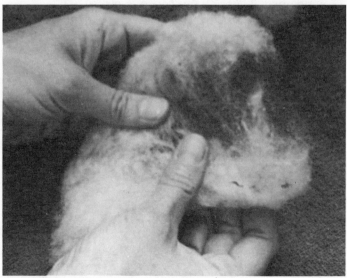

2 – Split this in half lengthwise, then split the halves in half.

3 – Finally, split the quarters in half lengthwise, ending with eight very wispy, 5- to 6-inch pieces.

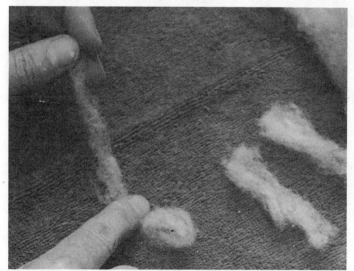

4 – Roll each piece slightly between the palms, then fold both ends of each piece over the center. Give each piece a little twist in the middle. Make enough of these for 1 round — 6 to 18, depending on the size of what you're making.

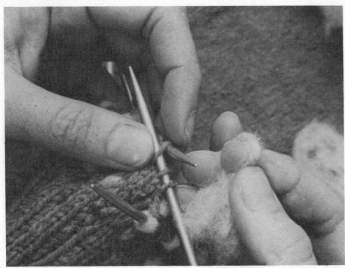

5 – Take a prepared bit of fleece, give it a couple of good twists in the middle, and hold it over one forefinger.

7 – Now, wrap the yarn over the needle too (or pick it up with the needle), locking the fleece in place.

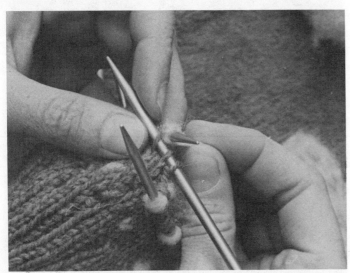

6 – Slip the needle in under the twist and lift it off the finger. Keep a constant hold on the ends so the fleece doesn't come untwisted.

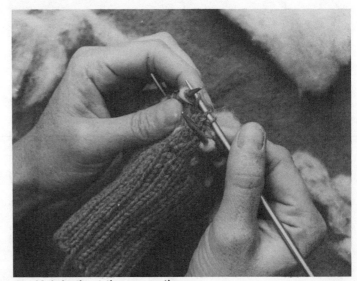

8 – Knit both at the same time.

Fleece-stuffed Mittens

Materials: 3 to 6 ounces worsted weight, oily natural yarn. 1 ounce 1-inch rovings or natural carded fleece in a contrasting color.

Equipment: 1 set no. 5 dp needles or size needed to obtain correct gauge. One set no. 3 dp needles for ribbing. Yarn needle for finishing.

Gauge: 4½ sts = 1 inch, measured across the round with fleece.

Sizes: Child's 2- to 4-year-old (child's 6 to 8 years, adult's small, adult's medium, adult's large). These are not sized to be shrunk but are actual sizes.

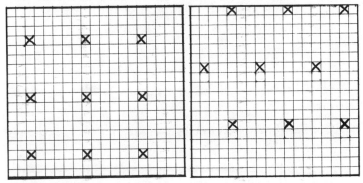

Pattern: A multiple of 6 sts and 6 rounds, it can be knit flat if desired. A bit of contrasting fleece is knit into the fabric along with the yarn every sixth st of every sixth round. Fleece sts can be arranged to form vertical lines (left) or diamonds (right).

To prepare bits of fleece: Judy McGrath of Happy Valley, Labrador, recommends taking a bit of roving or fleece about 5 to 6 inches long (and about ⅛ the width of the 1-inch roving, very thin and light) rolling it only slightly between the palms to shape it, then folding both ends over the center and giving it a couple of twists in the middle.

To knit fleece: Insert needle in next st to k, lay twisted bit of fleece over inserted needle with ends to the inside, then wrap yarn as usual, knitting both fleece and yarn in the same st. The yarn locks the fleece in place. When wrapping the yarn, try to avoid laying it so that it will show on the front of the fabric. If it does, the fleece can be pulled forward with a yarn needle later, but why make extra work?

Cuff: On no. 3 dp needles, cast on 33 (36, 39, 45, 48) sts. K 2, p 1 for 2½ (2¾, 3, 3½, 4) inches.

Change to no. 5 dp needles. K 1 round.

Insert first fleece in next round and follow fleece pattern from there on. Be sure there is fleece covering every square inch of the inside, especially the tips of the fingers and thumb. This will mean inserting fleece along the lines of decrease and other unlikely places. If you don't have a multiple of 6 sts, improvise a little on the pattern on the palm side.

At beginning of second round, p 1, k around to 4 sts shy of this p; and p 1, inc 1 in next st, k 1, inc 1 in next st, p 1. The p st should line up with the one from the preceding round and form a line on each side of the thumb gore.

Inc 1 on both sides of the thumb gore, within the marking p sts, every 4th round 3 (4, 4, 5, 5) times total. There should be 9 (11, 11, 13, 13) k sts between the p sts, and the thumb gore should be about 2 (2¼, 2¾, 3, 3) inches long, measured along the line of p sts.

Put 9 (11, 11, 13, 13) thumb gore sts on a string. Cast on 3 to bridge the gap and k straight up 1½ (2½, 2¾, 3, 3½) inches for the hand.

Lay mitten flat with the thumb either in toward the palm or sticking slightly out to the side. Mark the point on the needles corresponding to the 3 sts just above the thumbhole. You will dec on either side of these 3 sts. Now mark the 3 sts on the exact opposite side of the mitten from these 3. This will also be a dec line.

Dec this round, and every second round, on both sides of these two marking lines of 3 sts by knitting 2 together. Stuff this part of the mitten as generously as the pattern permits, and be sure there is fleece up in the very tip of the mitten and up the marking lines on both sides. Be generous.

When 16 to 20 (depending on size) sts remain, cast off, break yarn and weave tail back and forth across mitten tip to imitate a row of stockinette knitting. Then work the tail into the back of fabric.

Thumb: Pick up from string 9 (11, 11, 13, 13) sts, 1 st from each side of hole, and 3 sts from top of hole. Total 14 (16, 16, 19, 19) sts. K straight up 1¼ (1½, 1¾, 2, 2¼) inches. Dec sharply (never forgetting to stuff, of course). K 2, k2 together first round, then k 1, k 2 together until only about 6 sts remain. Break yarn, draw up remaining sts on the tail firmly, then darn smoothly back and forth over the tip.

Now, turn mitten inside out. First work all tails into the back of the knit. Then, using your fingers, carefully pick at all the fleeces, fluffing them apart but not pulling them loose, trying to spread the fluff evenly over the inside surface. This process will be completed by the wearer of the mitten.

Fleece-stuffed Cap

Fleece-stuffed Caps are made by the craft cooperative in Cartwright, Labrador, to match their Stuffed Mittens. As far as I know, they have no traditional history, but are delightfully warm, if a little bulky-looking.

Because of the thickness of the fleece lining, the actual hat circumference is 2 inches larger than usual for each size. Thus, a toddler's would be 18 rather than 16 inches, a child's 20 rather than 18, and an adult's can measure 22 to 24 at the brim edge.

There is no pattern here for an infant's stuffed hat as all that fleece might prove more than a baby could handle.

Materials: 3 to 4 ounces worsted weight yarn, depending on size. 1½ to 2 ounces 1-inch roving or carded, natural, oily fleece in a contrasting color.

Equipment: 1 set long no. 5 dp knitting needles (or regular no. 5 knitting needles, if knit flat), or size needed to obtain correct gauge. 1 set no. 3 dp (or straight) knitting needles for ribbing.

Gauge: 4½ sts = 1 inch measured on the round with fleece inserts.

Sizes: Child's small (child's medium, adult's medium, adult's large).

Pattern and instructions for preparing fleece: see Stuffed Mitten pattern.

If knitting flat, p every other row and add an extra st at end of each row for the seam.

Cuff: On no. 3 dp knitting needles, cast on 81 (88, 100, 108) sts. K 2, p 2 straight up for 3½ (4, 4½, 4½) inches.

Change to no. 5 needles. Inc 4 (2, 2, 0) sts, evenly spaced. K 3 rounds before inserting first fleece. Follow pattern from that point, being careful to continue stuffing with fleece all the way to the tip, even if the pattern must be compromised slightly when decreasing.

K straight up in pattern 3½ (4, 4½, 5) inches.

Begin dec: K 7 (8, 9, 10) sts, k 2 together, repeat around. Decrease at the same points every fourth round once, every third round twice, every second round once, then every round until only 20 to 22 sts remain. Break yarn, draw up remaining sts firmly on the tail. Run tail through the remaining sts twice more, then darn the end into the fabric. Darn other end into the cuff invisibly.

Now, turn the cap inside out and, using your fingers, pick and fluff the fleece bits to make them wider and flatter. Make a pompom for the tip, if you want.

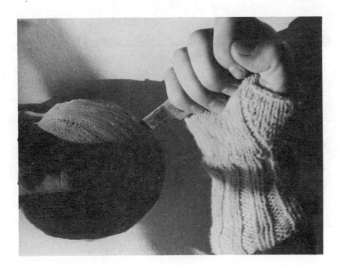

Wristers

Wristers are cuffs without mittens, usually about 5 inches long, extending in under the sleeve and out under the mitten, sometimes with a little loop to secure them to the thumb.

At one time most Maine mittens were knit without stretchy cuffs, as are many in this book. The cuff was separate, a Wrister, and stayed on even when a man had to take off his mittens in the woods to do a fine adjustment on a bit of harness or a tool.

Wristers have also been called "pulse warmers."

About the only place Wristers are still used in Maine is on boats off the coast. Even Maine coast fishermen who have gone over to insulated gloves often still use Wristers in cold weather to protect their wrists from chafing by the edges of their frozen oilskin jackets. Laura Ridgewell, wife of West Point fisherman Bob Ridgewell, says Wristers prevent "pinboils" on the wrists.

Laura knits Wristers of Bartlettyarns 3-ply fishermen's yarn, a naturally oily cream-colored yarn, on no. 5 double-pointed needles. For the instructions to work, one must have a gauge of 5½ sts per inch.

Instructions are given for child's 6 to 8, with instructions for adult's small, medium, and large in parentheses.

On no. 5 dp needles, cast on 33 (36, 39, 42) sts. K 2, p 1 for 3½ (4, 4½, 5) inches. Bind off in rib. Don't break the yarn, but using a size K crochet hook, make a chain about 2 inches long coming from the edge of the cuff. Attach this again at a point 2½ (2¾, 3, 3¼) inches from its beginning. Some knitters might go over this with a finer quality fishermen's yarn in buttonhole stitch to make it last longer and chafe less.

Phyllis Wharton of Seal Harbor sent me another kind of wrister, which she knits for her grandson and other scallop fishermen. This is the wrister shown in the photograph: essentially a mitten without a thumb or finger coverings.

Mrs. Wharton uses Bartlett yarns 2-ply fisherman yarn and no. 4 double-pointed needles. If you want the cuff a little tighter, use no. 2 or 3 needles for the cuff only. Cast on 39 sts and k 2, p 1 for 30 rounds (3½ inches). Change to no. 4 needles, transfer the last p st to the first needle, p 1, inc 1 in the next st, k 1, inc 1 st in the next st, p 1, and knit around. Maintaining the 2 p sts as markers, inc 1 st each side of thumb gore within the markers 5 times — once each 3 rounds. Total 12 sts between p sts. K 2 more rounds. Cast off 12 thumb gore sts and cast on 3 sts over the gap in the next round. K straight up 6 more rounds (¾-inch) and cast off tightly. Make another.

The Nova Scotia Museum published the following description (which is not quite a pattern) and have kindly given me permission to reprint it.

Nippers are made by knitting a 6-inch long cylinder of plain stocking stitch on a set of 4 double-pointed needles. A strip of very heavy cotton is folded and sewn in the centre. The ends of the cylinder are folded towards the middle and the two side folds are filled with fleece. The two ends are then sewn together. Nippers are still worn today by some Nova Scotia fishermen. (Joleen Gordon, et al., *A Nova Scotia Work Basket*, [Halifax: The Nova Scotia Museum, 1976.], p. 14)

Nippers

Ask a Maine fisherman about Nippers today, and he'll probably tell you he doesn't use them. The hydraulic trap hauler, a noisy but useful machine, has taken over most of the line hauling for fishermen, and what's left doesn't require Nippers.

A Nipper looks like two stuffed tubes of knitting attached together along one side and at both ends. They were slipped on, one to a hand, over the palm, and cushioned the hand against the bite of the rope while actually providing more fetch and grip than the hand can manage on a narrow line.

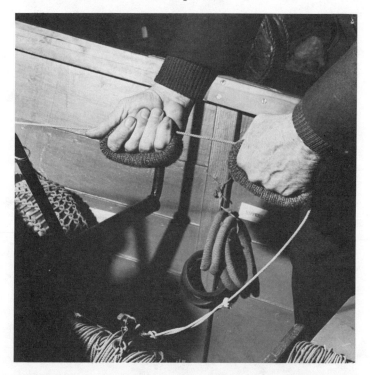

Nippers in use. (Courtesy of the Nova Scotia Museum.)

Part Two

Double-knit Mittens From Up-country

Double-knit Mittens from Up-country

From Maine to Newfoundland and Labrador, there's a tradition of double-knitting mittens — that is, knitting two strands of contrasting colored yarn alternately to form a pattern on the surface of the fabric. This makes a mitten which has the thickness but not the bulkiness of two mittens. Some of the patterns of alternation pull up the fabric into ridges, increasing the thickness even more.

Double-knit Mittens could be knit in one color with two strands of yarn, but that would be confusing to the knitter, and would also deny the knitter a chance to create beauty out of the tedium of family knitting. The New England housewife has never denied herself the right to make her handwork beautiful.

Long ago, patterns of colors evolved to be used exclusively for mittens, patterns that both thicken the fabric and allow the knitter to play with color.

These patterns are carried down within families and among friends, often with descriptive names and stories attached to their design or origin. Mattie Owl's Patch, Fox and Geese, Jacob's Ladder, and Snowflakes are only a few.

The patterns of color and the details of knitting each mitten are passed along with great precision. Most of the mittens here are in the Anglo-Maine tradition: they have rounded tips and thumbs, rather than what Maine women call "pickèd" tips (pronounced almost like "picket" fence). All have a small all-over design rather than having one design on the palm and another on the back like Norwegian mittens, and all have a triangle of increases to make room for the thumb, unlike Maine and Canadian mittens in a French tradition, which don't allow extra stitches for the thumb. All the mittens here are decreased at the tip in such a way that there is really no left or right mitten; the mitten can be "trained" to either hand or left ambidextrous.

Many of the patterns are regional within the Maine-Canadian Maritimes area. In St. Anthony's, Newfoundland, for example, the inside of the thumb is always knit in a vertical stripe. A St. Anthony's woman was amused when I showed her a mitten knit entirely in vertical stripes, a fairly common traditional pattern in Maine.

The Fox and Geese pattern is knit in Maine, Nova Scotia, and New Brunswick, but is almost unknown in Labrador, as is Labrador's Diamond pattern in Maine. A single family in Cape Breton, Nova Scotia, has knit a version of the Labrador diamonds for over a hundred years, because a fisherman in the family found and liked such a mitten while fishing on the Grand Banks in 1858. (Story from Gordon, *A Nova Scotia Workbasket*.)

Some of the patterns have very precarious existences. Mariner's Compass, a pattern somewhat difficult to work with because it's based on a multiple of eight stitches (rather more than usual), was knit in Harpswell, Maine, as well as Barrington, Nova Scotia, until fairly recently. Janetta Dexter, a collector of double-knit patterns in Nova Scotia, told me the same pattern is occasionally knit in New Brunswick, where it's called Spider Web, and in Liscomb County, Nova Scotia, where it's called Mattie Owl's Patch. Mrs. Dexter calls it Naughts and Crosses in her book. Although it's very like Fox and Geese, its bulkiness for knitters has confined it to tiny corners of the area, to individual women here and there who are willing to put up with its drawbacks.

The pattern is no longer knit in Harpswell. It was almost lost in Liscomb County. An Indian woman, Mattie Owl, called one evening some years ago at the home of a Liscomb County woman who knit mittens for her family. Mattie Owl was wearing an incredibly ragged pair of mittens, which had been patched with scraps from another handknit, made in the Mariner's Compass pattern. The woman liked the pattern so much that she traded Mattie Owl a pair of new mittens for the patched pair. The pattern has been knit in the family now for three generations, called after its origin, Mattie Owl's Patch. (Story told to me by Janetta Dexter, summer 1982.)

The patterns and the style of knitting that accompanies them probably date back to the early British settlers in New England and the Maritimes. But their warmth and the simplicity of their designs fit well into modern northern life. They're easy to make and strikingly good-looking.

General Instructions for Double-knitting

When I started knitting Scandinavian sweaters and such, I found that the knitted fabric I produced was lumpy and tighter than my regular (beautiful) knitting. To prevent the tightness, I tried using a larger size of needle. I correctly guessed the lumpiness was because the strand not in use was pulled too tightly on the back of the fabric. To prevent this I looped the yarn around the needle an extra time for every other change of color, then went back and evened up every row before going on, suspecting meanwhile that there might be an easier way.

The back of my wondrous double-knitting showed all the extra lengths of yarn between stitches in neat

little twists, because I had read somewhere that one should always pick up the new color from beneath. Because every action has an equal and opposite reaction, and every twist I put into the knit caused an opposite one in the yarn, I had to stop every once in a while and dangle the piece of knitting from its yarn while it gently swirled in the air and untwisted itself.

All this suffering was unnecessary. If someone had only told me, or showed me — if some instructions had only shouted at me, "Pay attention!" — I would have known the solution, long before Nora Johnson showed me. Double-knits can come off needles perfectly flat, with even tension, with exactly the same number of stitches you planned on and no twists in the back or in the yarn.

The first axiom is: **Never twist the yarn.** Pick up one color, the lighter one, from above, and the darker color from beneath. The darker color will stick out a little from the surface of the knit, but it will do so consistently. And it will look good.

The back of the fabric will have straight lines as regular and neat as the design on the front.

In Maine and the Maritimes, this technique is called "carrying the main color ahead," because the dark strand is picked up from underneath and from ahead — in the direction of knitting — of the light strand. The light strand is always brought around (and above) the dark strand; it appears from the knitter's viewpoint to be slipping around from behind when it's picked up.

The Norwegians do this by holdng the dark strand on their left forefinger and the light strand on their right forefinger. Then they knit with a combination of English and continental knitting, wrapping the yarn with their right finger and picking it off their left. You can do the same if you wish.

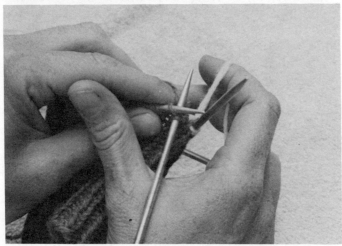

In Norwegian stranding, the dark strand is held on the left forefinger; stitches are picked off with the needle when needed. The light strand is carried on the right forefinger, and stitches are wrapped around the needle as in American knitting. This keeps the two strands separate — the dark on the bottom (but emphasized on the surface of the knitted fabric) and the light on top (but seemingly in the background of the knitted fabric).

In continental two-strand knitting, the dark strand is carried near the second joint of the left forefinger, the light nearer the tip. Although both strands are picked up in exactly the same way, their relative positions keep the dark strand beneath and the light above and prevent twisting while emphasizing the dark color on the fabric surface.

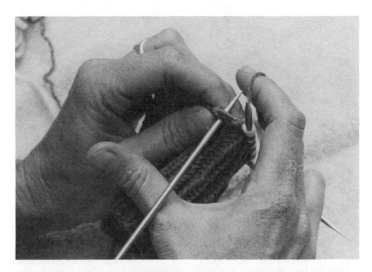

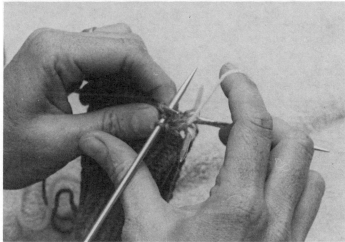

In ordinary, old-style American knitting (for want of a better name), the dark strand can be emphasized and the strands kept separate by always picking up the dark strand from in front of the light and always bringing the light strand around (and above) the dark. This is awkward, but it works. Some knitters use the middle finger to catch up the light strand and the forefinger for the dark. (The last two fingers pinch both strands and control tension for all these methods.)

If you knit continental style, lay the dark color near the joint of your left forefinger, the light strand nearer the tip. Pick them both up the same way.

Those of us who knit in the old way can use the forefinger to pick up the dark color, which is ahead, and the middle finger for the lighter color.

The second axiom is: **Make sure to check the tension of your knitting in the double-knit pattern you're using.**

Some of the patterns are meant to pull up tightly. They will have to be knit on a larger needle than others that don't pull up but call for the same number of stitches per inch. I've adjusted for this in the patterns here, but make sure you knit the same tension as I do, or the pattern won't come out the right size. See the general instructions on how to make a test gauge.

Increasing: Almost all the double-knit mittens here have a thumb gore made by adding a whole pattern element at once in the center of the thumb gore, usually in the first pattern row. That is, instead of adding 2 stitches on each side of the thumb gore every 2 or 3 rows, you add 6, dead center, every sixth round for patterns based on a multiple of 6 stitches, or 4 every fourth round, for patterns based on a multiple of 4 stitches, and so forth. This is done on the same pattern round on each band of pattern until there are enough stitches for the thumb. Surprisingly, it makes a very gentle, hand-shaped thumb and is not as sudden as it sounds. It's also easier to remember when to increase.

Because a lot of increase stitches must be packed into a very short distance — six increases in the space of three stitches, for example — several different techniques are often used together.

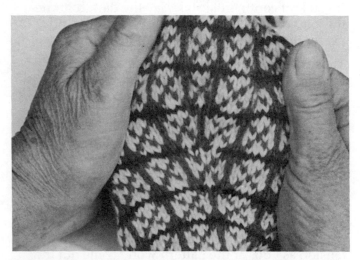

In most cases, stitches are increased on the thumb gore a whole block at a time, right in the middle of the thumb gore. In Fox and Geese, a pattern with a multiple of 6 stitches, a whole block of 6 stitches is added at the horizontal line between band of pattern. There are 3 such increases in this picture.

A common way to increase in these mittens is to increase at a point where the color changes, knitting both colors simultaneously into one stitch in the right order for the pattern. In the next round, each color is knit as a stitch. There are two such increases already knit on the right needle.

In the first, the two different-colored strands of yarn are knit into the same stitch at the same time, taking care that they lie on the needle in the correct order to fit the pattern. In the next round, each color is knit as a separate stitch.

In the second, the yarn is knit into the back of a stitch from the preceding round.

In the third, the yarn is simply wound around the needle as if to knit. In ordinary stockinette stitch this would leave a hole, but here there is tension on the back of the stitches from the other strand of yarn carried behind the work, and the increases are crowded closely together. This increase doesn't leave a hole in these mittens.

In the fourth, the yarn is knit, between stitches, into the strand of the color carried on the back in the preceding round.

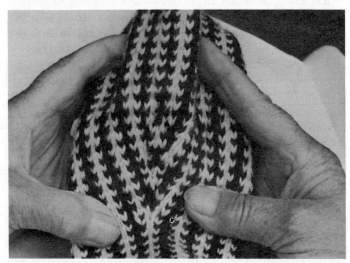

In Spruce, 4 stitches are added in the center of the thumb gore every 4 rounds, ideally forming a series of V- shapes.

The most commonly used techniques are the first and third.

Decreasing: The width of the knit is decreased by knitting 2 or 3 stitches together, depending on the pattern.

On mittens with linear patterns, this is usually done at both ends of the needle, in every round. The result is a mitten tip with three, usually distinct, decrease lines, none falling on the edge of the hand. Mittens with such a tip can be worn on either hand so that wear is evened out somewhat and the mitten lasts longer.

To decrease on patterns based on squares, at least one whole pattern element is dropped once each band by knitting 2 stitches together as many times as there are stitches in the square.

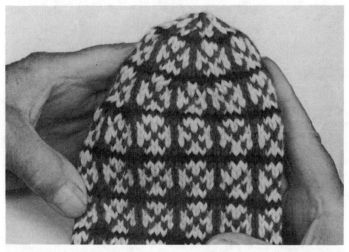

In patterns with blocks, some decreases are made by knitting 2 stitches together as many times as there are stitches in a block. For Fox and Geese, here, with 6 stitches to a block, 12 stitches are knit together, 2 by 2.

Cuffs: At least in the southern half of Maine, double-knit mittens often have an unribbed cuff, knit in a pattern of vertical stripes, which fits very snugly on the wrist. Women I've talked to in northern Maine and in the Canadian Maritime Provinces knit ordinary ribbed cuffs and don't recognize the snug vertically striped ones.

Because they are comfortable, and because they are specifically from Maine, I've included these snug cuffs in several patterns, with an option to make a regular cuff. In the area where these mittens are knit, a regular ribbed cuff is made by knitting 2 and purling 1 around, or by knitting 3 and purling 1. This is said to grip the wrist better than the knit 2, purl 2 or the knit 1, purl 1 traditional in the rest of the United States.

The snug cuffs are knit in a two/two (or one/one) alternation of colors, which makes vertical stripes in stockinette st. To prevent the edge from curling, a different method of casting on is used, which I have called "the Maine method."

The yarn is cast on double with a twist added to each stitch. Each stitch is pulled up very tightly from both sides just after it's cast on. Study the photo series on the subject.

Casting on

When casting on for snug Maine cuffs, use a double strand of yarn, once and a half as long as your reach. Hold the strands taut with the last fingers of the left hand and follow the motions in the pictures.

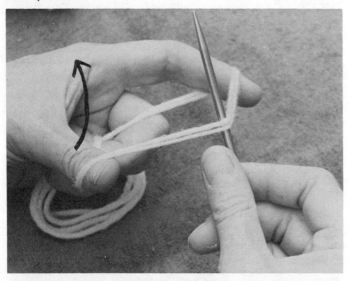

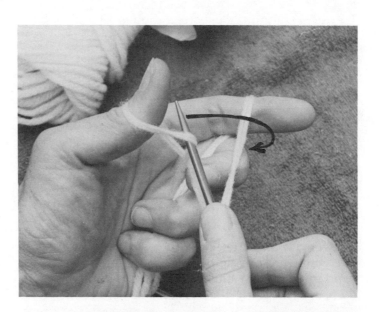

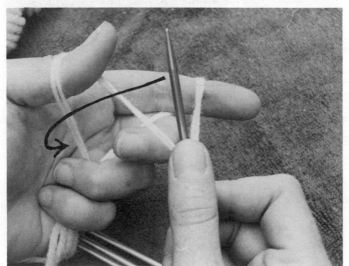

When you reach this point, the left thumb and forefinger let go, and the needle pulls toward the body. The first cast-on operation makes 2 stitches. Succeeding ones make only 1. (If you're not making snug Maine cuffs and are casting on with a single strand, you can use this method for all the stitches.)

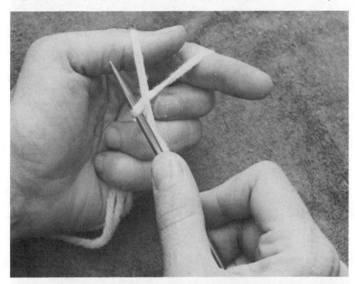

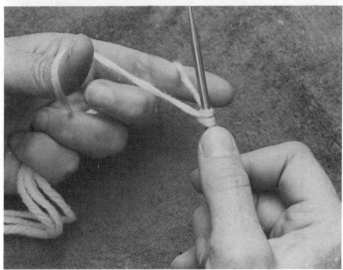

Casting on — the Maine method

To cast on by the Maine method, start with 1 (or 2) stitches already cast on halfway down a double length of yarn half again as long as your reach. Follow the photo series closely.

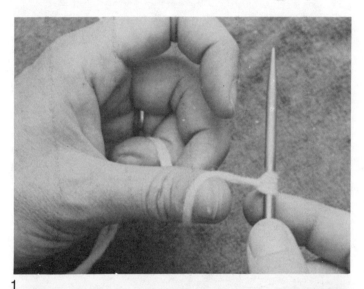

1

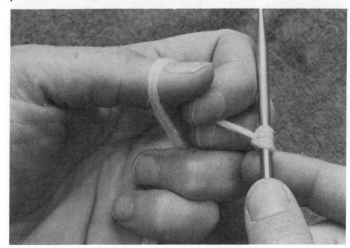

2

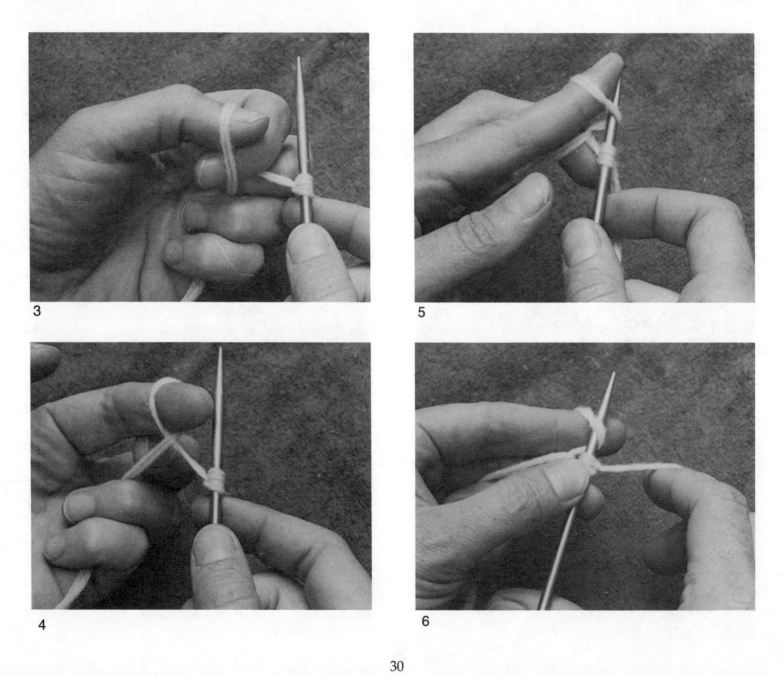

3

4

5

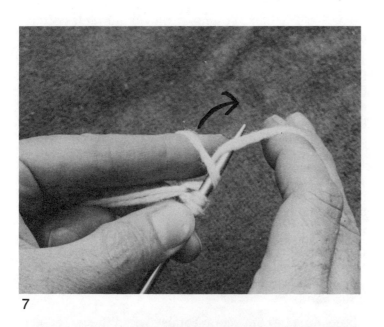

7

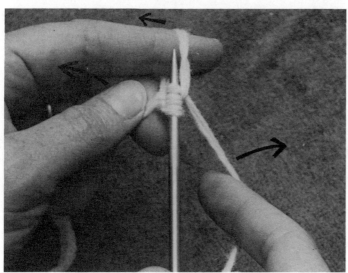

8

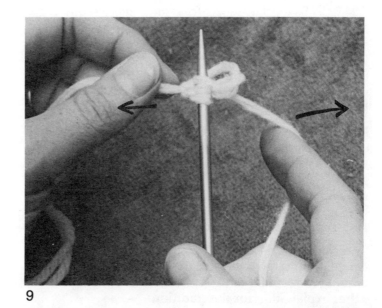

9

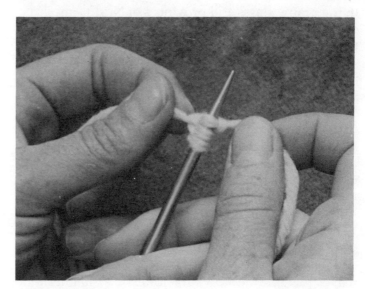

Be sure to pull the yarn up tightly on both sides of each stitch, or the edge of the cuff will curl outward.

Fox and Geese Mittens, Cap, and Shooting Gloves

In Anglo-Saxon farm lore, foxes and geese seem to go together as easily as crackers and cheese or cats and mice. We own an old baby spoon decorated on the handle with the incised figures of a goose frantically fleeing a pursuing fox. There are quilt patterns and mitten patterns called Fox and Geese which seem to have no relation to either animal pictorially.

My friend Tony Cary of Bath pointed to the back wall of her fireplace and told me the weather — rainy for a week — would clear, because there were no fox and geese there. She explained the Mainers call the moving sparks on the back of the fireplace and the bottom side of the woodstove lid "fox and geese," and that they portend bad weather.

Tony said that as a girl she had imagined light catching on the wings of night-flying geese in the waving movement of the sparks, but she has no other explanation for the tradition.

In the prairie states and provinces of North America, children stamp a crossed circle into the snow, then play a chasing game called "Fox and Geese·" The crossed circle shows up again in an old handmade game from the Maritime Provinces, also called "Fox and Geese." The Fox and Geese Mitten pattern, rendered in two colors, as it is in Canada, looks like the crossed circles of the Fox and Geese games.

Mainers, not knowing the game, had to be more inventive. Nora Johnson of Five Islands, who learned to knit these mittens as a girl in the Farmington area, told me the only "real Fox and Geese Mittens" have three colors: red for the horizontal lines, black for the verticals and crosses, and white for the background.

Knitting the design in three colors completely destroys any resemblance to the Fox and Geese games, but makes possible the story Mrs. Johnson's grandmother told her — that the design actually depicts foxes and geese. To see them, you must allow your fantasy free play.

The red lines are fences; the little black dots forming the X's are worried little geese with their wings flapping. At the corner of each box, looking through the fences, is a fox's head, its ears (which could also be geese) pointing diagonally up, and its nose pointing straight down. Work on it. If you want to, you'll be able to see them.

This pattern is based entirely on Mrs. Johnson's pattern, although I have worked out more sizes based on her verbal instructions.

Roughly, you add one more block around and one more band in finger length for each size increase. The thumb grows from three blocks around for very young children to five blocks around for men with large hands.

There must be some compromise when the increase is a minimum of three-quarters of an inch. Florence Nowell of Newport reduces a too wide thumb by ripping it out and reknitting with needles one size smaller. Don't try this on small children's sizes, which tend to be narrow enough.

Fox and Geese Mittens

Materials: In Maine, Fox and Geese Mittens are traditionally knit with black verticals and crosses, a white background, and red fences. Depending on size, use 1 to 3 ounces black, 1 to 3 ounces white, and about 1 ounce red worsted weight yarn.

Equipment: 1 set no. 4 dp knitting needles, or size needed to obtain correct gauge.

Gauge: 7 sts = 1 inch in pattern.

Sizes: Child's 2 to 4 (6 to 8, women's small, women's medium, men's medium, men's large).

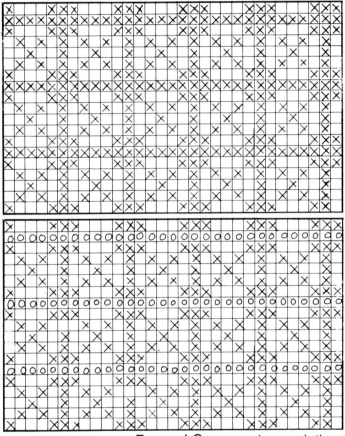

Fox and Geese — two variations

Pattern: A multiple of 6 sts and 6 rounds; incs and decs are almost only made in the first round. For clarity, 1 band means all 6 rounds; 1 block means all 6 sts.

First round: k 1 black, k 3 white, k 2 black around.

Second round: k 1 white, k 1 black around.

Third round: k 2 white, k 1 black around.

Fourth round: k 1 white, k 1 black around.

Fifth round: k 1 black, k 3 white, k 2 black around.

Sixth round: k in red around.

Note: Carrying the third color is a bit of a problem, simplified somewhat if one uses a bobbin or a fishermen's netting needle for the red. Drop it down inside the mitten when not using it.

This pattern can't easily be knit flat.

Be sure to read General Instructions for Double-knitting before starting this project.

Cuff: With double strand of black yarn and using Maine method, cast on tightly 36 (42, 48, 54, 60, 66) sts on 3 no. 4 dp needles, 12 (14, 16, 18, 20, 22) per needle.

Start pattern immediately. K 2 (2, 3, 3, 3, 3) bands. End in red. The vertical black lines (foxes' noses) behind the red fence will be visible now as well as groups of 5 little geese fluttering nervously in an X formation.

Thumb gore: For left mitten, inc will be in this round at vertical, 2 blocks before end of round. For right mitten, 2 blocks after beginning of round. This puts the joint of the pattern on the palm.

Inc (left mitten): K 1 block, *k 1 black, k 2 white. K both strands into the next st, first white then black, without twisting the st. Loop the black yarn as if to k before the next st. K both strands, black then white, into the next st. Loop the white yarn as if to k, then knit both strands into the next st, white then black. Loop the black yarn as if to k, then k the next st black as usual.* K around in pattern. You have now done the seemingly impossible feat of increasing 6 sts in the space of 3.

Inc (right mitten): K up to first st of second-to-last block, then k * to *.

Complete the band, then inc the same way in the 1 black and 3 white sts above the newly added block. The black and white will be reversed from the first time. This will cause a black vertical to rise from between the verticals of the first new block and give a total thumb gore inc of 12 sts.

Complete this band. For child's 2 to 4 (6 to 8) the thumb gore is finished. Skip the next two paragraphs.

For women's small or medium, k the next band without an inc. Skip the next paragraph.

For men's medium and men's large, inc again around the new black vertical, duplicating the first inc instructions. Total inc should be 18.

In red round, and before knitting them, put 11 (11, 14, 14, 19, 19) thumb gore sts onto a string or yarn holder, taking extra sts from the next block on the palm side of mitten. Keep the black vertical next to the thumb on the back of the hand intact; don't put it on a string!

Cast on over thumb hole 5 (5, 8, 8, 9, 9) sts in red.

Hand: K up 2 (3, 4, 4, 4, 5) bands.

For child's sizes 2 to 4 and 6 to 8, skip next two paragraphs.

For women's small and medium, in first round, k 2 together 6 times on side opposite thumb. One block will disappear. For women's small, skip next paragraph.

For women's medium and men's medium and large, complete band, then dec 2 blocks by knitting 2 together 6 times on front and back of mitten, starting with second vertical after thumb edge and second vertical after little-finger edge.

On round 5 of band, k 2 together black, *k 1 white, k 2 together in white, k 1 black, k 2 together in black*. Repeat * to * around.

On red round, k 1, k 2 together. Repeat around.

Next round, start as if starting pattern again, lining up verticals with earlier ones wherever possible.

Next round, k 1 white, k 2 together in black. Continue this until 8 or 9 sts remain. Break yarn. Draw remaining sts up on 1 strand, then darn end invisibly back and forth through tip, making it smooth and rounded. Avoid a point at the tip.

Thumb: Put on 2 needles the 11 (11, 14, 14, 19, 19) sts from string. K them in red. Pick up 1 st from side of hole in appropriate color, then pick up 5 (5, 8, 8, 9, 9) sts from top of hole, matching colors to pattern so that verticals seem to pass behind the red fence uninterrupted. This is tricky but can be done. Pick up last st from other side of hole, in correct color for pattern.

There should be 18 (18, 24, 24, 30, 30) sts, all arranged properly to continue knitting 3 (3, 4, 4, 5, 5) blocks. Complete first round.

Note: Because the pattern limits the choice of widths for the thumb, the thumb may be slightly too loose or too tight when completed. If so, take it out and re-knit with a needle one size larger or smaller.

K straight up in pattern 1½ (2, 2, 2½, 3, 3) bands. Then k 1, k 2 together, either in red or in alternating black and white, whichever fits into the pattern.

With 8 sts remaining, break yarn. Thread 1 strand into darning needle and draw up remaining sts. Darn invisibly back and forth over the tip to make a tip that looks and feels smooth and rounded. Avoid a point or a knob.

Work all remaining tails into the back of the knit.

Checkerboard, Sawtooth
and Fox & Geese mittens

Fox & Geese shooting gloves

Checkerboard mittens and cap

Spruce mittens and cap, baby's Fox & Geese mittens and cap

Top Checkerboard mittens,
bottom Salt and Pepper mittens

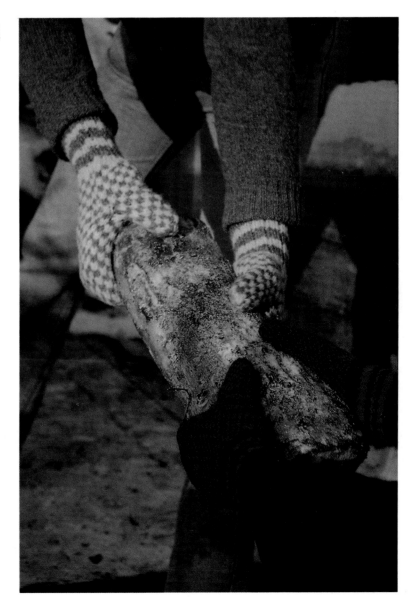

Fox & Geese pattern in two colors

Baby's helmet and mittens,
Spruce pattern

Left Fleece-stuffed mittens
and cap, *right* Sawtooth
mittens and cap

Fox and Geese Cap

Materials: 3 ounces dark, 1 ounce light, and 1 ounce red (if desired) worsted weight yarn.

Equipment: 1 set no. 5 dp needles for ribbing; 1 set no. 8 dp needles, or size needed to obtain correct gauge. Yarn needle for darning in ends.

Gauge: 5½ sts = 1 inch in pattern; 5 sts = 1 inch in plain stockinette st.

Sizes: 1- to 3-year-old child (3- to 6-year-old child, adult). This corresponds to a final hat measurement of 16 (18, 20) inches. A knitted cap should be from 2 to 5 inches smaller than actual head measurement.

Pattern: See Fox and Geese Mittens for pattern and pattern notes.

Starting from the cuff and using no. 8 dp needles, cast on 90 (96, 108) sts with dk yarn. Change to no. 5 dp needles and k 1, p 1 for 4 rounds.

Change to no. 8 dp needles. If using red, k 1 round red, then knit Fox and Geese pattern, preferably in purl.

Knit 2 bands of pattern, ending with 1 round in red or dk.

Change to no. 5 needles and k 1, p 1 for 9 rounds.

Change to no. 8 needles and stockinette st. K 2 together 8 (6, 8) times, evenly spaced. K straight up for 4¼ (4½, 4¾) inches.

Dec: K 10, k 2 together, repeat around.

K 2 rounds.

K 9, k 2 together, repeat around.

K 2 rounds.

K 8, k 2 together, repeat around.

K 2 rounds.

K 6, k 2 together, repeat around.

Add pattern: k 3 lt, k 4 dk (catching up lt twice behind work). Repeat around.

K 1 dk, k 1 lt, k 1 dk, k 1 lt, k 2 together dk, k 1 lt. Repeat around.

K 1 lt, *k 1 dk, k 2 lt*. Repeat * to * around.

K 1 dk, k 1 lt around.

K 1 lt, k 2 together lt, k 1 dk, k 2 together dk. Repeat around.

K 1, k 2 together around in dk, until about 32 sts remain.

Break the yarn about 8 inches long, and thread the dk tail through the remaining sts with a yarn needle and draw them up firmly. Draw the tail through the remaining sts twice more, then darn back and forth over the tip to reinforce it. Work all ends into the back of the fabric.

Fox and Geese Shooting Gloves

Shooting gloves of one sort or another are used all over the cold part of the northern hemisphere. Essentially, they are a mitten with a separate trigger finger; they combine the cozy finger-togetherness of mittens with the convenience of gloves.

They are not unique to Maine, although I have never seen *patterned* shooting gloves outside the Maine-Maritimes area.

This pattern was suggested by a Barlettyarns pattern for Fox and Geese Shooting Gloves, or Hunter's Mittens. It's not exactly the same pattern.

Materials: 2 to 3 ounces dark and 2 to 3 ounces light worsted weight wool yarn; 2 ounces red, if desired.

Equipment: 1 set no. 2 dp knitting needles for ribbing, 1 set no. 4 dp knitting needles or size needed to obtain correct gauge. Yarn needle to work in ends.

Gauge: 7 sts = 1 inch.

Sizes: Child's 6 to 8 (women's small, women's medium, men's medium, men's large).

Pattern: See adult Fox and Geese Mittens for pattern and pattern notes.

Cast on 48 (48, 54, 60, 66) sts in dk yarn on no. 2 dp needles. K 2, p 1 for 2½ (3, 3, 3, 3½) inches, striping, if desired, every few rows with lt.

Change to no. 4 dp needles, k 1 round in dk. Start pattern immediately, k top half (whole, whole, whole, whole) band of pattern.

Thumb gore: For left mitten, inc will be in the first pattern round at the vertical, 2 blocks before the end of the round. For the right mitten, 2 blocks after the beginning of the round. This puts the joint in the pattern on the palm.

Inc (for right mitten): K 1 block, k 1 dk, k 2 lt. *K both dk and lt strands into the next st, first lt, then dk, without twisting the st. Wrap dk yarn as if to k. K both strands into the next st, first dk then lt, without twisting. Wrap lt yarn as if to k. K both colors, lt then dk, into next st. Wrap dk yarn as if to k.* K the next st as usual in dk. K around in pattern.

Complete the band, then inc the same way (from * to *) in the 1 dk and 3 lt sts above the newly added block. The dk and lt will be reversed from the first time. This inc will cause a black vertical to rise between the verticals of the first new block and will give a thumb gore inc of 12 sts.

Complete this band. For child's 6 to 8, the thumb gore is finished. Skip the next two paragraphs.

For women's small and women's medium, k the next band without an inc. Skip the next paragraph.

For men's medium and men's large, inc again around the new black vertical, duplicating the first inc instructions (* to *). Total inc should be 18.

In red round, and before knitting them, put 11 (17, 17, 23, 23) sts onto a string, taking extra sts from the next block on the palm side of mitten. Keep the black vertical next to the back of the thumb intact; don't put it on a string!

Cast on over thumb hole 5 sts in red.

K straight up in pattern 2 (2, 2½, 2½, 3) bands of pattern. Take off 11 (11, 17, 17, 17) sts onto a string for trigger finger. For child's 6 to 8 and women's small, take 4 sts from the back and 8 over the thumb. For other sizes, take 1 whole block from the back, and 2 from over the thumb.

Cast on 5 sts over gap and k straight up in pattern for 2½ (3, 4, 4, 5) bands.

For child's size 6 to 8, dec starting with pattern round 3: *K 1 dk, k 2 together lt,* repeat * to * around. Next round, repeat first round. Next round, k 2 together around. Skip next three paragraphs.

For women's small and medium, in first round, k 2 together 6 times on little-finger side, starting with a dk vertical. 1 block will disappear. For women's small, skip next paragraph.

For women's medium and men's medium and large, complete band, then dec 2 blocks by knitting 2 together 6 times on palm and back of mitten, starting with the first vertical after thumb side and second vertical after little-finger edge.

On round 5 of band, k 2 together dk, *k 1 lt, k 2 together lt, k 1 dk, k 2 together dk,* repeat * to * around.

On red round, k 1, k 2 together, repeat around.

Next round, start as if starting pattern again, lining up verticals with earlier ones wherever possible.

Next round, k 1 lt, k 2 together dk. Continue this until 8 or 9 sts remain. Break yarn. Draw remaining sts up on 1 strand, then darn smoothly and invisibly back and forth through tip. Avoid a point.

Trigger finger: In correct color, pick up 11 (11, 17, 17, 17) sts from string, 2 from each side of the hole, and 5 between fingers for 3 (3, 4, 4, 4) blocks around. For child's 6 to 8 and women's small, it's impossible to get the pattern to match here. Sacrifice the match between the fingers. K straight up in pattern until 4 (5, 5, 5½, 6) inches above thumb hole.

Dec sharply: K 1, k 2 together (trying at first to maintain dk verticals) until 6 to 9 sts remain. Break yarn, draw remaining sts onto lt strand, and darn smoothly and invisibly back and forth over tip.

Thumb: Put on 2 needles the 11 (17, 17, 23, 23) sts from string. K them in red. Pick up 1 st from side of hole in appropriate color, then pick up 5 sts from top of hole, matching colors to pattern so that verticals seem to pass behind the red fence uninterrupted. This is tricky but can be done. Pick up last st from other side of thumb hole in correct color for pattern.

There should be 18 (24, 24, 30, 30) sts, all arranged properly to continue knitting 3 (4, 4, 5, 5) blocks. Complete first round.

Note: Because the pattern limits the choice of thumb widths, the thumb may be slightly too loose or too tight when completed. If so, take it out and re-knit with a knitting needle one size larger or smaller.

K straight up in pattern 2 (2, 2½, 3, 3) bands. Then k 1, k 2 together all the way around, either in red or in alternating black and white, whichever fits into the pattern.

Continue, keeping as closely as possible to pattern, until 8 sts remain. Break yarn. Pull remaining sts up on lt strand and draw up firmly. Darn invisibly and smoothly back and forth over the tip.

Work all remaining tails into the back of the knit.

Striped Mittens and Cap

One of the first Maine double-knit mittens I ever saw was a Striped Mitten, but the pattern is less popular than either the Fox and Geese pattern or the Salt and Pepper pattern. This may be because the sharp lines of the pattern emphasize any mistakes the knitter might make.

To the careful knitter, however, the sharp lines are the pattern's best asset, because they also emphasize perfection and yield a fine mitten with enough fashion pizzazz to be at home in London or Boston.

The pattern, a simple one-one alternation of two colors, pulls the mitten fabric up into fine ridges making it appear that one color has been knit above the other. They are traditionally knit with a dark color "on top" and a very bright, warm color showing through from underneath.

A friend of mine, seeing a pair like this, exclaimed, "Just like hot coals!" What more could one ask of a mitten color than that they look warm enough to be coals?

This pattern was shown to me by Nora Johnson of Five Islands. She learned it as a girl in the Farmington area. It was until recently also knit by Elma Farwell of the Dromore area of Phippsburg. It seems to be unknown outside of Maine.

Striped Mittens

Materials: 2 to 3 ounces each dark- and light-colored worsted weight yarn.

Equipment: 1 set no. 4 dp knitting needles, or size needed to knit correct gauge.

Gauge: 7 sts = 1 inch in one-one pattern.

Sizes: Child's 2 to 4 (child's 4 to 6, child's 8 to 10, women's small, women's medium, men's medium, men's large).

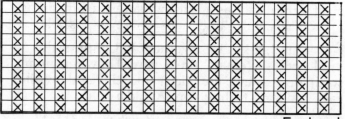

For hand

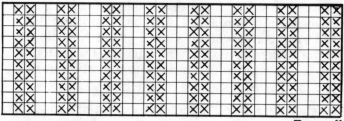

For cuff

Patterns: Cuffs: k 2 dk, k 2 lt. Hand and thumb: k 1 lt, k 1 dk.

Based on a multiple of 2 sts and 1 row, this pattern can be knit flat but add 1 additional st each side for the seam. Note: Read General Instructions for Double-knitting before starting.

Cuff: Using double-strand dk yarn and Maine method, cast on 36 (40, 44, 48, 52, 56, 60) sts.

Start cuff pattern immediately and k 2 dk, k 2 lt for 2¼ (2½, 2¾, 2¾, 3, 3, 3) inches.

In the next round, start the thumb gore and the pattern for the hand and thumb.

Thumb gore: Nora Johnson of Five Islands makes a very striking beginning to her striped thumb gore, which looks as if three narrow dark stripes branch out from one of the wide dark ones on the cuff. To get this effect, you'll have to cheat a little, as follows:

Start the thumb gore at the beginning of the round, above 2 dk sts. K both colors, dk then lt, into the first dk st; wrap the dk yarn around the needle as if to k; then k both colors into the next dk st, first lt then dk. The cheating part is that you now have an uneven number of sts, and the pattern won't work. So, k 1 lt, then k 2 sts together in dk, and everything's all right again. K 1 dk, k 1 lt around.

K 2 rounds in pattern without increasing.

On third round, inc 4 sts, 2 in each outside dk stripe of the thumb gore: k both colors (dk then lt) into the dk st from the preceding round, then, k 1 dk st into the dk st from the present round. K 1 lt, k 1 dk, k 1 lt, and inc 2 more in the next dk st the same way. There should now be the beginning of 2 dk Y-shapes with a lt st emerging in the middle of each.

Inc this way every fourth round 2 (3, 4, 4, 5, 5, 5) times. K 4 more rounds.

Put 9 (13, 15, 15, 19, 19, 19) thumb gore sts on a string, leaving a dk st at each edge of the hole. Cast on 5 (5, 5, 5, 5, 7, 7) sts over the gap in the correct color sequence, starting with a lt st.

K straight up in pattern 2¼ (3, 3½, 3½, 4, 4, 4½) inches.

Start dec: Figuring out the dec for the Striped Mittens is a bit of a Chinese puzzle. Even people who knit these mittens sometimes wonder how they do it, so don't be alarmed if you have a little trouble. The idea is that the dark lines should dominate right up to the tip. Look at the diagrams and read the instructions.

First, be sure each needle begins with a dk st and ends with a lt one, that there are about the same number of sts on each needle, and that one needle covers the center back.

First dec round (A): K together in dk the second to last pair of sts on the first needle, starting with a dk st; then k 1 dk, k 1 lt. At the beginning of the next needle, k together in dk the second pair of sts, starting with the second dk st. Do the same with the other 2 needles.

Second dec round (B): You will have 2 pairs of dk sts together on each needle. At the end of the first needle, k in dk the first of the dk pair, without dec. K the next dk st together with the next lt st **in lt**. End of needle. At the beginning of the next needle, k the first dk st together with the first lt st, in dk. K the next (dk) st in lt. Repeat this on the other 2 needles.

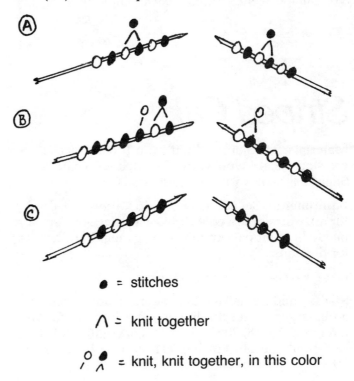

Ⓐ

Ⓑ

Ⓒ

● = stitches

∧ = knit together

○ ● = knit, knit together, in this color
∕ ∧

43

Continue alternating these 2 rounds until there are only about 12 sts left. Then break yarn, draw the dk tail through the remaining sts and pull up firmly. Darn the dk tail back and forth across the tip as invisibly as possible.

Thumb: Pick up and k 1 dk st from side of thumb hole, 9 (13, 15, 15, 19, 19, 19) sts from the string, 1 dk st from the other side of the hole, and 5 (5, 5, 5, 5, 7, 7) sts from the top of the thumb hole.

K straight up in pattern 1¼ (1½, 2, 2, 2¼, 2¼, 2½) inches, then dec sharply: K 1 lt, k 3 together dk until only 6 to 8 remain. Break yarn and draw these up firmly on the tail on 1 strand, using a yarn needle. Darn this strand back and forth across the tip.

Work all loose ends into the back of fabric.

Striped Cap

Materials: 2 to 3 ounces of dk and 1 to 2 ounces lt worsted weight wool yarn, if knitted with cuff. Slightly less dk yarn if knitted as pictured.

Equipment: 1 set 10-inch no. 6 dp knitting needles (or no. 6 straight needles if working flat), or size needed to knit pattern in correct gauge. Yarn needle for finishing.

Gauge: 6 sts = 1 inch in pattern.

Sizes: Child's small (child's medium, adult medium, adult large), corresponding to a finished cap circumference of 16 (18, 20, 22) inches. For comfortable fit, a cap should be 2 to 4 inches less than the head circumference. Adult medium fits most people.

Pattern: K 2 dk, k 2 lt on a multiple of 4 sts. This is the same pattern used for snug cuffs, but it's not used for the whole striped mitten. Be sure you've read General Instructions for Double-knitting before you begin.

If knitting flat, purl every other row and read the pattern from right to left on purl rows. Add 1 extra st to each end of the work for the seam.

On 3 no. 6 needles, cast on 96 (108, 120, 132) sts in dk, using a double strand and the Maine method (see under General Instructions for Double-knitting: cuffs). Start pattern immediately.

K straight up in pattern for 5½ (6, 6½, 6½) inches.

(This cap, as pictured, has no cuff. If you want to make a man's cap with a cuff, cast onto no. 4 needles 96 (108, 120, 132) sts with a single strand of dk yarn, then k 1, p 1 for 3 (3½, 4, 4) inches. Change to no. 6 needles and k 2 dk, k 2 lt straight up for 3¾ (4½, 5, 5) inches. Then follow the rest of the instructions.)

Dec: K 2 dk, k 2 lt together in lt. Repeat around.

K 9 rounds of k 2 dk, k 1 lt, then dec again: k 2 dk, *k 1 lt and l dk together in dk yarn, k 1 dk*. Repeat * to * around. There's no more stripe.

K 3 more rounds in dk, then dec again: k 3 together around until only 20 sts remain.

Break yarn and pull up the remaining sts firmly on both strands using a yarn needle. Thread the tail through these sts once more, then darn each strand individually into the inside of the tip. Work all other loose ends into the back of the fabric.

Make a big pompom for the tip or hang a tassel made from the dk yarn from the tip by a 2-inch-long string of crocheted chain st.

Salt and Pepper Mittens and Cap

Salt and Pepper, a simple one-one alternation of two colors, must be the granddaddy of the double-knit patterns. It's definitely the most common double-knit in Maine, and in the whole Maine-Maritimes area, it is the most widespread.

In the Maritime Provinces, Salt and Pepper is rarely used for the whole mitten as it is in Maine, but when calculation of a pattern doesn't fit neatly into a space, as on the thumb or the mitten tip, the knitter often lapses into Salt and Pepper. In Maine when such problems arise, the knitter usually knits plain, dropping the second color, but then it's a lot colder in Newfoundland and Labrador.

Called Salt and Pepper in Nova Scotia, it's properly called Snowflake in Maine, when it's called anything. Often knitters here have scoffed at my interest in names. "I didn't do anything, just knit it double," they have said more than once of their Salt and Pepper mittens.

In fact, no double-knit pattern is simpler or more effective. The alternation on an uneven number of stitches produces a fish-scale appearance and a dense, smooth fabric with easy mobility and no inside loops to catch the fingers.

The mitten is usually knit with a dark or dull color emphasized and a glowing warm red or orange underneath. It's also traditionally knit in gray and white — more natural but also much less dramatic.

Salt and Pepper Mittens

Materials: Depending on size, 2 to 3 ounces dark, and 2 to 3 ounces light, worsted weight wool yarn.

Equipment: 1 set no. 4 dp knitting needles or size needed to obtain gauge. 1 set no. 2 dp knitting needles for ribbing on cuff (optional).

Gauge: 7 sts = 1 inch.

Sizes: Child's 2 to 4 (child's 4 to 6, child's 8 to 10, women's small, women's medium, men's medium, men's large).

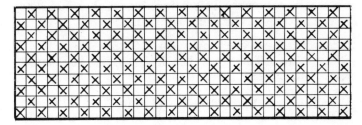

Pattern: A multiple of 2 sts and 2 rounds, knit on an uneven number sts. The pattern can be knit flat. The uneven number of sts insures that the alternation will form checks rather than stripes. (Note: Be sure to read General Instructions for Double-knitting before starting this project.)

First round: K 1 dk, k 1 lt.

Second round: K 1 lt, k 1 dk.

Cuff: Using a single strand of dk yarn and the Maine method, cast on tightly 36 (40, 44, 48, 52, 56, 60) sts, dividing these equally among 3 no. 2 needles.

K 3, p 1 in dk for 2½ (2½, 3, 3, 3, 3, 3) inches. Change to no. 4 needles.

(The cuff can also be knit in pattern by casting onto no. 4 dp needles using a double strand of yarn and the Maine method. K 2 dk, k 2 lt for the same lengths as indicated above. This will make a snug cuff with 2-st-wide stripes.)

Start pattern and inc 3 (3, 3, 3, 1, 1, 1) sts, evenly spaced, in the first round.

Thumb gore: At beginning of next round, inc 4 sts: k both colors into the first st. Do not twist sts. Repeat in next 3 sts. Put a marker on the needle just after the last inc.

Complete round and next 3 rounds.

At beginning of next round, inc 2 sts the same way. Then k in pattern to 2 sts before the marker. Inc 2 sts in the next 2 sts, the same way.

Make this inc every fourth round a total of 3 (3, 4, 4, 5, 5, 6) times. Total incs: 12 (12, 16, 16, 20, 20, 24) sts. K ¾-inch up with no inc 0 (0, 1, 1, 1, 1, 1) times.

Put onto a string or yarn holder 11 (11, 15, 15, 19, 19, 23) thumb gore sts. In pattern, cast on over thumb hole 5 (7, 5, 5, 5, 7, 5) sts.

Hand: K straight up in pattern 1¾ (2½, 3¼, 3½, 3¾, 4, 4¼) inches.

Narrow off: Dec 4 sts each side each round by knitting 3 together on opposite sides. Always start dec with a dk st and try not to line decs up with a dec in the previous round. It's okay if the decs wander all over the tip of the mitten, but try to balance them one to a side in each dec round.

After first half-inch of dec, dec 2 at both ends of each needle by knitting 3 sts together, repeating until only 8 to 12 sts remain.

Break yarn and draw these sts up on the dk strand, using a yarn needle. Darn the tail invisibly back and forth through the mitten tip, making a smooth finish. The tip should be rounded, without a knob in the fabric.

Thumb: Pick up and k from string 11 (11, 15, 15, 19, 19, 23) sts. K 1 in pattern into the side of the thumb hole, pick up and k 5 (7, 5, 5, 5, 7, 5) sts from the top of thumb hole, and k 1 into the other side of the thumb hole. There should be no break in the pattern.

Total 18 (20, 22, 22, 26, 28, 30) sts. K 2 together at the beginning of the second round to make the number uneven.

K straight up 1¼ (1½, 2, 2, 2¼, 2¼, 2½) inches, then dec sharply: k 1 dk, k 3 together (dk, lt, dk) in lt, every other round until only 6 to 8 sts remain.

Break yarn, draw up remaining sts on the dk strand, and darn tail smoothly and invisibly back and forth across the tip. Tip should not look pointed.

Work all other tails into the back of the fabric.

Salt and Pepper Cap

Salt and Pepper is a smooth, non-bulky double-knit that can be knit into the crown of any cap with a plain-knit crown. For a lighter feel, the extra color could be knit in every other round.

Materials: 2 to 3 ounces dk and 1 to 2 ounces lt worsted weight wool yarn.

Equipment: 1 set 10-inch no. 7 dp knitting needles (no. 7 straight needles if knitting flat) or size needed to knit pattern in correct gauge. 1 set 10-inch no. 4 dp (or straight) knitting needles for ribbing. Yarn needle for finishing.

Gauge: 6 sts = 1 inch in pattern.

Sizes: Child's small (child's medium, adult medium, adult large), corresponding to a cap measuring 16 (18, 20, 22) inches around. For a good fit, caps should be 2 to 4 inches smaller than the circumference of the head.

Pattern: See Salt and Pepper Mitten instructions for pattern and pattern notes.

If working flat, purl every other row and read pattern right to left on purl rows. Add 1 more st to both ends for the seam.

Read General Instructions for Double-knitting before starting.

Cuff: On no. 4 needles, cast on 96 (108, 120, 132) sts in dk. K 1, p 1 for 3 (3½, 4, 4) inches.

Change to no. 7 needles and start pattern, adding 1 st in first round by knitting both colors into 1 st. K straight up in pattern for 3¾ (4½, 5, 5) inches.

Adjust sts so that there is an equal number on each needle (except one), each needle beginning with a dk st and ending with a lt st.

Dec: Dec 4 sts each needle by knitting 3 sts (dk, lt, dk) together at both ends of each needle. The dec st will be made with lt yarn.

K 4 (4, 5, 5) rounds in pattern.

Repeat dec round.

K 2 (2, 3, 3) rounds.

Repeat dec round.

K 1 (1, 2, 2) rounds.

Repeat dec round, then k every round as a dec round until only 18 sts remain.

Break yarn and pull up remaining sts firmly on both strands. Thread the tail through these 4 sts once more, then darn each strand individually into the back of the tip. Work all other loose ends into the back of the fabric.

Attach a single-colored pompom to the tip if you want to.

The cuff should be turned up about half its length, so that it also forms the inside band of the cap.

Spruce Mittens and Cap

This pattern appeared in an old Bartlettyarns catalog, nameless except for the designation "patterned mitten." The instructions didn't include a thumb gore or a double-knit thumb. When I began to knit the pattern in green on a white background, it looked like a spruce or fir twig, so I decided to call it that.

When I showed the finished mitten to Janetta Dexter, who collected many Nova Scotia double-knitting patterns, she said it is also knit there and called Jacob's Ladder. A variant, appropriately called False Jacob's Ladder is knit by alternating rows of 1 lt, 2 dk, 1 lt with rows of 2 lt, 2 dk.

Call it what you like, it's a striking pattern.

The increase at the thumb gore is in the middle of the thumb gore rather than at the sides, based on Nora Johnson's Fox and Geese pattern and Bida Spooner's Checkerboard pattern.

Spruce Mittens

Materials: Depending on size, 2 to 3 ounces dark- and 2 to 3 ounces light-colored worsted weight yarn. The traditional colors, if any exist for this pattern, are unknown to me, but it looks handsome in white with a dark green pattern.

Some knitters find Spruce too "busy" in contrasting colors. If you agree, try it in complementary colors like blue-gray and gray, maroon and dark pumpkin, or light and dark gray.

Equipment: 1 set no. 5 dp needles, or size needed to obtain correct gauge. Yarn needle for darning in ends.

Gauge: 7 sts = 1 inch.

Sizes: Child's 2 to 4 (child's 4 to 6, child's 8 to 10, women's small, women's medium, men's medium, men's large).

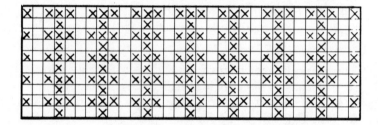

Pattern: A multiple of 4 sts and 2 rounds. This pattern can be knit flat if desired, but an extra st should be added at each side for the seam. (Note: Be sure to read General Instructions for Double-knitting before starting this project.)

First round: K 1 lt, k 3 dk around.

Second round: K 2 lt, k 1 dk, k 1 lt around.

Cuff: Using double strand of light yarn and Maine method, cast on tightly 36 (40, 44, 48, 52, 56, 64) sts, dividing these equally among 3 no. 5 dp needles. Start pattern. K straight up for 2½ (2½, 3, 3, 3, 3, 3) inches. Begin thumb gore in next round.

Thumb gore: Choose a point to start the thumb gore, preferably 2 to 3 patterns from the beginning of the round and so that the joint at the beginning of the round falls on the palm. Use the center of the lt vertical as a center line for the first inc, and inc in the first pattern round when there are 3 dk sts.

Now, approaching the single white st, k both colors into what should be the last dk st, first dk, then lt. Wrap dk yarn as if to k. K 1 dk into the next st without an inc. (It will be directly above the lt center st from the previous round.) Wrap dk yarn as if to k,

48

then k both strands into the next st, first lt, then dk, without twisting. You're there. Total 4 incs.

The inc stays in the center and will form a series of V-shapes in the pattern, alternating dk and lt.

Inc this way (reversing colors) every third round 3 (3, 4, 4, 5, 5, 6) times for a total inc of 12 (12, 16, 16, 20, 20, 24) sts. K up without increasing 0 (0, ¾, ¾, ¾, ¾, 0) inch.

Put on string 11 (11, 15, 15, 19, 19, 23) sts of the inc sts. Cast on 7 sts over the thumb hole, maintaining the correct sequence of colors. Pattern should meet correctly at the other side of the gap.

Hand: K straight up in pattern 1¾ (2½, 3¼, 3½, 3¾, 4, 4½) inches.

Dec: Lay mitten on palm with the thumb against the palm. One dk vertical will run from the cuff edge just past the back of the thumb gore. Maintain this and the 2 lt center lines on either side of it as a dec marker all the way to the tip. Do the same on the opposite dk and 2 lt center lines.

Starting at one of these dk dec lines, k 2 in pattern, k 1 lt, and k next 2 sts together. *K across in pattern to 2 sts before next lt dec line. K these 2 sts together. K 5 sts in pattern (decrease column), k next 2 sts together* Repeat * to * every round.

After 1 inch of dec rounds, k 4 together in center of palm, starting with lt st in first pattern round. 1 dk vertical should disappear.

(An easier but less handsome way to dec: shift sts so that each needle has about the same number of sts and begins with a lt center st. One needle should cover the whole center back. Now k 2 together twice at both ends of all 3 needles every other round twice, then every round, maintaining pattern all the way.)

Continue to dec until there are only 10 to 12 sts remaining. Break yarn and draw up remaining sts on the tail of one strand. Darn this end back and forth invisibly over the tip. The tip should be slightly rounded, not pointed, and should feel smooth and flat.

Thumb: Pick up from string 11 (11, 15, 15, 19, 19, 23) sts. K 1 in pattern into the side of the thumb hole, pick up 7 sts from the top of thumb hole, and k 1 in pattern into the other side of thumb hole, keeping pattern intact all the way. The pattern should follow up from the hand perfectly on all sides. Total 20 (20, 24, 24, 28, 28, 32) sts.

K straight up 1¼ (1½, 2, 2, 2¼, 2¼, 2½) inches, then dec quickly starting with first pattern round: k 1 lt, k 1 dk, k 2 together in dk, k 1 lt around. Next round: K 1 lt, k 2 dk together dk. Maintain the dk center until there is an alternation of 1 lt, 1 dk, then dec every st, knitting entirely in lt yarn. Break yarn, drawing up remaining sts on the lt strand. Darn back and forth over the tip with the lt yarn for a smooth, rounded finish.

Work all tails into the back of the fabric.

Spruce Cap

Materials: 2 to 3 ounces lt and 1 to 2 ounces dk worsted weight wool yarn, depending on size.

Equipment: 1 set 10-inch no. 6 dp knitting needles (no. 6 straight needles if knitting flat), or size needed to knit pattern in gauge. 1 set 10-inch no. 4 (or straight) knitting needles for ribbing. Yarn needle for finishing.

Gauge: 6 sts = 1 inch in pattern.

Sizes: Child's small (child's medium, adult's medium, adult's large), corresponding to caps 16 (18, 20, 22) inches in circumference. Knitted caps fit best if 2 to 4 inches less than the circumference of the head. Most people can wear the adult's medium.

Pattern: See Spruce Mitten instructions for pattern and pattern notes.

If knitting flat, purl every other row, reading pattern right to left. Add 1 more st to each end for the seam.

Read General Instructions for Double-knitting before starting.

Cuff: In lt, cast on 96 (108, 120, 132) sts, dividing them equally between 3 no. 4 needles. K 1, p 1 for 2¾ (3½, 4, 4) inches.

Change to no. 6 needles and k 1 round in lt.

Start pattern. K straight up in pattern 3¾ (4½, 5, 5) inches. End with second pattern round (1 dk, 3 lt). Adjust sts so there are center lt sts at the beginning of each needle.

Dec round: K first 2 sts together (in dk this time); k second 2 sts together in dk. K in pattern up to fourth st from end of needle (which should be lt st this time). K it and the next st together in lt; k the next 2 sts together dk. Repeat this on the next 2 needles.

The idea is to knit 8 sts (2 whole patterns) together to make 4 sts (1 whole pattern) at each intersection of the needles, thus eliminatng 3 patterns or 12 sts in each dec round. The pattern must be maintained all the way. *K 1 round, then repeat dec round.* Repeat ** once more, then k dec round every round now until only 20 sts remain. You will have to change the order of lt and dk sts each round. Just keep knitting in pattern — it'll work.

Break yarn and pull up remaining sts firmly on both strands. Thread the tail through these sts once more, then darn each strand individually into the back of the tip. Work all other loose ends into the back of the fabric.

Attach a single-colored pompom to the tip, if you want.

The cuff should be turned up about half its length, so that it also forms the inside band for the cap.

Sawtooth Mittens and Cap

I first saw this pattern in a 1908 Priscilla Knitting Book published in Boston. It looked so in tune with Maine double-knit patterns that I took it for one.

I later learned that Sawtooth is knit throughout Nova Scotia and New Brunswick even today. And my Maine informant, Nora Johnson, said her mother used to knit the pattern in the Farmington area. I've never seen a native Maine edition of it, but assume it must be a pattern lost during this century.

The "teeth" of the Sawtooth pattern can be made in various sizes, from a multiple of five stitches in width down to three stitches in width for baby mittens. It's also fun to decrease at the tip of the fingers and thumb by reducing the size of the sawteeth.

The traditional colors for this mitten are bright red and gray. Every example I've seen, even the 1908 picture, has been in these colors.

The pattern is based loosely on the Priscilla Knitting Book pattern and on examples lent by Janetta Dexter and the Nova Scotia Museum. Although the knitting book pattern has a striped thumb, certain technicalities of the pattern make it easier if the Sawtooth pattern is maintained throughout.

Adult's Sawtooth Mittens

Materials: 2 to 3 ounces gray and 1½ to 2½ ounces red worsted weight wool yarn.

Equipment: 1 set no. 3 dp knitting needles, or size needed to obtain correct gauge. 1 set no. 1 dp knitting needles for ribbing (optional). Yarn needle for finishing.

Gauge: 7 sts = 1 inch.

Sizes: Women's small (women's medium, men's medium, men's large).

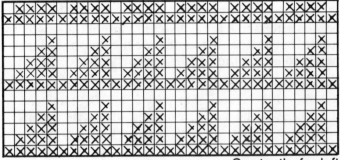

Sawtooth, for left

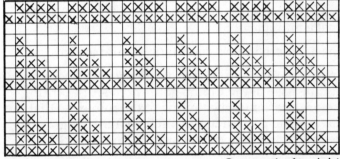

Sawtooth, for right

Pattern: A multiple of 5 sts and 6 rounds, this pattern can only be knitted flat if double-pointed needles are used.

Pattern for double-knit cuff: K 2 red, k 2 gray around.

Pattern for right mitten:

First round: K around in red.

Second round: K 1 gray, 4 red.

Third round: K 2 gray, 3 red.

Fourth round: K 3 gray, k 2 red.

Fifth round: K 4 gray, k 1 red.

Sixth round: K around in gray.

Note: All incs and most decs will take place in the second pattern round, which will be called the 1/4 round.

Some knitters like to reverse the slant of the sawteeth for the left mitten. If you do, use the graph shown here and adjust the written instructions accordingly.

Cuff: On no. 3 dp needles, cast on 48 (52, 56, 60) sts. K 2 gray, k 2 red straight up for 2¾ (3, 3, 3) inches. (Cuff can also be made by casting 48 (52, 56, 60) sts onto no. 1 dp needles in gray yarn, then k 3, p 1 for the same lengths as above. Stripe with red if desired.)

K 1 round in gray, adjusting +2 (+3, −1, 0) sts to make multiple of 5.

Start pattern in next round. (K around in red.)

In the first 1/4 round, start thumb gore. Choose point for the base of the thumb gore, 1 red stripe (or rib) before or after the beginning of the round, so that the joint of the pattern will be on the palm. K 1 gray, k 4 red up to the pattern block of the thumb gore base.

In next 5 sts, inc 5 sts: K both colors, gray then red, into the first st. Don't twist or k into the back of st. Now, loop the red yarn over the right needle as if to k, k 1 red into the next st. K both strands into the next st, first red then gray, loop red yarn again as if to k, k 1 red into next st, loop red yarn again, and k 1 red as usual. Total inc 5 sts. Continue to k 1 gray, k 4 red around. Complete band of pattern.

Inc as above 3 (4, 4, 4) times. Then k 1 band of pattern with no inc 1 (0, 0, 0) time.

On the next all-red round, and before knitting them, put 14 (19, 19, 19) thumb gore sts onto a string and cast on 4 (4, 4, 9) sts over the gap in red yarn. Finish the round.

K straight up in pattern 3 (3½, 3½, 4) inches.

Begin dec: At next 1/4 round, k 2 together 5 times over the 2-squares on the little-finger side.

At the next 1/4 pattern round, dec 2 squares: K 2 together 5 times on the little-finger side and 5 times on the thumb side. Complete the band.

At the next 1/4 round, dec 3 squares, evenly spaced. For the 2 men's sizes, complete the band and dec 3 more squares in the next 1/4 round the same way.

On the next 1/4 round for all sizes, dec the size of the sawtooth. K 1 gray, k 1 red, k 2 red together, k 1 red. Repeat around. Next round, k 2 gray, k 2 red. Next round, k 1 gray, k 2 gray together, k 1 red; repeat around. Next round: k around in gray: k 1, k 2 together, around.

In next round, k 1, k 2 together in red.

When there are only 10 to 12 sts remaining, stop decreasing, break yarn, and draw remaining sts up on the tail of 1 strand. Darn this tail invisibly and smoothly back and forth over the tip.

Thumb: Put 14 (19, 19, 19) sts from string onto 2 needles, pick up and k 1 st from side of thumb hole in gray, pick up and k 4 (4, 4, 9) sts from top of thumb hole in gray, and 1 st in gray from the other side of thumb hole. Then, k the 14 (19, 19, 19) sts from the string in red. K around in red (first pattern round), then continue pattern on total 20 (25, 25, 30) sts. (The pattern on the inside of the thumb will mirror the pattern beneath it on the palm. Don't be alarmed.)

K straight up in pattern 2 (2¼, 2¼, 2¾) inches. Dec sharply in the next 6 rounds to 8 to 10 sts. If 3 sts of the same color appear together, k 2 of them together around, decreasing the size of the sawtooth. At the gray line, k 2, k 2 together. Do the same with the red line.

When only 8 to 10 sts remain, break yarn, draw remaining sts up on the tail matching the last color used, and darn smoothly and invisibly back and forth across the tip. Avoid a knob on the tip.

Work all tails into the back of the fabric. Make another mitten.

Sawtooth Cap

Materials: 1 to 2 ounces red and 2 to 3 ounces gray worsted weight wool yarn, depending on size.

Equipment: 1 set long no. 6 dp needles, or size needed to obtain correct gauge. 1 set long no. 4 dp needles for ribbing. Yarn needle for finishing.

Gauge: 5½ sts = 1 inch.

Sizes: Child's small (adult's small, medium, large), corresponding to hats 16 (18, 20, 22) inches in circumference.

Pattern: See Adult Sawtooth Mittens for pattern and pattern notes.

Cuff: Cast on 88 (98, 110, 120) sts in gray yarn and no. 4 dp needles and k 1, p 1 for 3½ (4, 4½, 4½) inches.

Change to no. 6 dp needles and k 1 round in gray, adding 2 (2, 0, 0) sts, evenly spaced.

Begin pattern and k straight up in pattern for 3½ (4, 4½, 4½) inches.

Begin dec: On second pattern round, dec 2 squares (10 sts): K 2 together 5 times above 2 squares; repeat this on the other side of the cap. Finish pattern band.

Next second pattern round, dec 3 squares (15 sts) the same way. Complete pattern band.

On next second pattern round, dec 3 squares (15 sts) the same way. Complete band.

Next second pattern round, dec 4 squares; complete round, but not band. Third pattern round, k 2 gray, k 1 red, k 2 red together. Repeat around. Fourth pattern round, k 1 gray, k 2 together in gray, k 1 red. Next round, which will seem like the sixth pattern round but is only the fifth, k 1 gray, k 2 together in gray, repeating around. At end of round, change to red and continue to dec in pattern until there are 20 sts left.

Break yarn, draw remaining sts up on the tail of both strands firmly, then thread tail through sts once more. Darn each individually into the inside of the tip, reinforcing it.

Work all other loose ends into the back of the fabric.

Make a pompom for the top, if desired.

Child's Sawtooth Mittens

Materials: 1½ to 2 ounces gray and 1 to 1½ ounces red worsted weight wool yarn.

Equipment: 1 set no. 1 dp knitting needles for ribbing; 1 set no. 3 dp knitting needles, or size needed to obtain correct gauge. Yarn needle for finishing.

Gauge: 7 sts = 1 inch.

Sizes: Child's 2 to 4 years (6 to 8 years, 8 to 10 years)

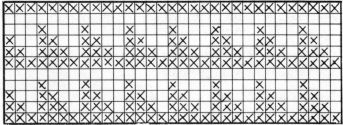

Child's sawtooth, for right

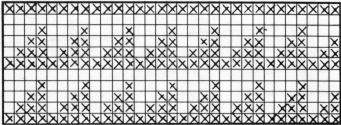

Child's sawtooth, for left

Pattern: A multiple of 4 sts and 5 rounds, this pattern can only be knit flat if double-pointed needles are used.

Right mitten:

First round: K around in red.

Second round: K 1 gray, k 3 red.

Third round: K 2 gray, k 2 red.

Fourth round: K 3 gray, k 1 red.

Fifth round: K around in gray.

Note: All incs and most decs take place in the second pattern round, which will be called the 1/3 round.

Some knitters like to reverse the slant of the sawteeth for the left mitten. If you do, use the graph shown here and adjust the written instructions accordingly.

Be sure to read General Instructions for Double-knitting before starting this project.

Cuff: On no. 1 dp needles, cast on 36 (40, 44) sts in gray yarn and k 2, p 2 straight up for 2¼ (2½, 2¾) inches. Add red stripes if desired.

(Cuff can also be made by casting onto no. 3 dp needles with a double strand of gray, using the Maine method. Then, k 2 gray, k 2 red for the same length. I've found, however, that these cuffs are a little too snug for children whose hands are at all wide or inflexible.)

Change to no. 3 needles and k next round in gray.

Start pattern in next round (k around in red).

In next round, the 1/3 round, start thumb gore. Choose a point for the base of the thumb gore, 1 red stripe or rib before or after the beginning of the round, so that the joint in the pattern will be on the palm.

K 1 dk, k 3 lt up to the pattern block of the thumb gore base. Inc 4 sts in the next 4 sts: K both colors, gray then red, into the st that should have been gray.

Don't twist or knit into the back of the st. Now loop red yarn over the right needle as if to k, then k the next st in red. K both colors, gray then red, into the next st, k 1 more red, loop red yarn over needle as if to k, then k the next st gray as usual. Total inc is 4 sts. Continue k 1 gray, k 3 red around. Complete band of pattern.

Inc this way 2 (3, 3) times. Then k 1 band of pattern with no inc 0 (1, 1) time.

In the next all-red round and before knitting them, place 7 (11, 11) thumb gore sts onto a string and cast on 7 sts over the gap with red yarn. Finish the round.

K straight up in pattern 1¾ (2½, 3) inches above the thumb hole.

At the next all-red round, dec 2 squares: K 2 together 4 times above 2 squares on the little-finger side. 1 square will disappear. Repeat on the thumb side.

At the next red round, dec 3 squares the same way, evenly spaced around the mitten. Don't finish the band of pattern.

On the 1/3 round, k 1 gray, k 1 red, k 2 red together. Repeat around.

On the 2 gray – 1 red round, k 2 gray together, k 1 red. In the next round (all gray) k 1, k 2 together all the way around. If necessary, continue to do so in the next round, which should be all red. When only 10 to 12 sts remain, break yarn, draw remaining sts up on the tail of 1 strand (whichever you ended with), and darn the end smoothly and invisibly back and forth over the tip of the mitten.

Thumb: Pick up 7 (11, 11) sts from string on 2 needles. Pick up and k 1 st from the side of the hole in gray; pick up 7 sts across the top of the thumb hole in gray (the pattern here will be upside down from the pattern on the hand), and 1 st in gray the far side of

the thumb hole. Total 16 (20, 20) sts. Knit around in red (pattern round 1).

K straight up in pattern 1¼ (1½, 2) inches.

Dec: Next time there are 3 sts of either color together, k 1, then k the next 2 of the same color together and repeat around. If this occurs again in the next 2 rounds, repeat the dec with the other color. If the next lines are solid, k 1, k 2 together around. In other words, dec sharply, down to 8 sts. Break yarn, draw the tail of the final color through the remaining sts, and darn it back and forth invisibly and smoothly over the tip.

Work all tails into the back of the fabric.

Make another.

Checkerboard Mittens and Cap

For those women who become tired of Salt and Pepper knitting, a one-one alternation of two colors that makes a smooth, thick mitten fabric, there's Checkerboard, also called Block or Two-Two but having nothing to do with trains.

Checkerboard is an alternation of colors in a two-two sequence — two rows of 2 dark, 2 light followed by two rows of the opposite. It shouldn't be very different from Salt and Pepper, but it is. For a reason known only to yarn engineers, this particular alternation pulls the fabric up into ridges like corn rows, thickening the mitten fabric greatly. It looks like a fancy stitch, but it isn't. It's just common old stockinette stitch.

Checkerboard is knit in central (Farmington) and northern (Aroostook County) Maine, as well as in New Brunswick and Nova Scotia. I've never seen a Checkerboard mitten from southern Maine, but that doesn't mean there aren't any.

Checkerboard can be knit with three stitches and three rows per check, or even with four stitches and rows, but the most common pattern has only two.

Three versions are presented here, one taken intact from a mitten in New Sweden, a lighter, easier to knit version like those seen in central Maine and New Brunswick, and a very light version in sport weight yarn for babies and young children (under Baby Foxes and Goslings).

The matching cap for the two heavier mittens is made with worsted weight yarn.

Incredible Checkerboard Mittens

These mittens are super — super thick, super warm, super solid, super flexible. They are a mitten once knit in northern Aroostook County for woodsmen, who wore them as liners under leather mittens.

The woman who gave me the pattern, Bida Spooner of New Sweden, told me she is Swedish. Both her mother and father were Swedish, she said. But the mitten she began to knit after she married is pure Anglo-Maine from its Checkerboard pattern to its rounded tips.

Mrs. Spooner is one of the few women I interviewed who still send fleeces to Bartlett Mills. Her son keeps and shears the sheep and takes the fleeces to Harmony, where he buys her gray and white natural yarn.

She washes the heavy 3-ply yarn in hot water in the skein, then winds it for her winter knitting. Mrs. Spooner has a local reputation for her mittens and was a little afraid that publishing her instructions might damage her business.

However, in spite of the simple and curious manner of putting on the thumb gore (all at once, at the bottom), it's not an easy mitten to knit because of the thickness of the yarn and the tightness of the knit. But it's well worth the effort to knit a pair, though only in Bartlettyarns 3-ply Homespun Yarn, pre-washed in hot water!

Materials: 3 ounces gray and 3 ounces white 3-ply Homespun from Bartlettyarns, Harmony, Maine. This yarn is about half again as heavy as regular knitting worsted.

Equipment: 1 set no. 8 dp knitting needles, or size needed to knit gauge. 1 set no. 5 dp knitting needles for ribbing. Yarn needle for finishing.

Gauge: 6 sts = 1 inch in pattern.

Sizes: Women's large or men's medium.

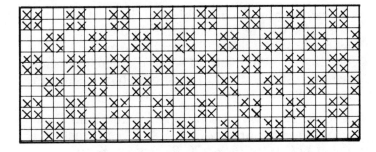

Pattern: A multiple of 4 sts and 4 rounds. This pattern can be knit flat if an extra st is added at each end for the seam.

First round: K 2 dk, k 2 lt.

Second round: Same as first.

Third round: K 2 lt, k 2 dk.

Fourth round: Same as third.

Note: See General Instructions for Double-knitting before starting.

Cuff: In gray, cast on 36 sts, dividing them equally between 3 no. 5 dp knitting needles. K 2, p 1 in gray for 7 rounds, white for 3 rounds, gray for 4 rounds, white for 3 rounds, gray for 4 rounds, and white for 3 rounds.

Change to no. 8 dp needles. K 1 round white, picking up the little loop between every pair of k sts, and thus inc 4 sts per needle. Total 48 sts.

Choose a point to start the thumb gore: For the left mitten, 2 k ribs before the end of the round; for the right mitten, 2 k ribs after the beginning of the round. In the first 2 pattern rounds, you will inc 12 just above 6 sts there. That will be the only thumb gore inc.

Start pattern: K 1 gray, *k 2 lt, k 2 gray* repeating * to * around.

At the thumb gore point, k both colors into the second gray st, first gray, then white. In the next st, repeat, but first white, then gray. In the third st, repeat, but gray, then white. In the fourth st, repeat, but white, then gray. K the next st gray. This will make 4 new sts. Repeat this in the second pattern round but do it in 8 sts for a total of 12 inc sts.

K straight up in pattern a total of 7 two-round bands (14 rounds). Put 19 thumb gore sts on a string, cast on 3 over the gap. Inc 4 above these 3 sts in the next round and continue in pattern for 12 more 2-round bands.

Begin dec: K to 3 sts before end of first needle. *K 2 together in pattern, k 1. On next needle, k 1, k 2 together, in pattern, and k to 3 before the end of that needle.* Repeat from * to * on every needle, maintaining the check as best you can, until only 10 to 12 sts remain.

Break yarn, draw up these sts on 1 strand, then darn this smoothly back and forth through the tip.

Thumb: Pick up and k 19 sts from string, make another st in the side of the thumb hole in the correct color, pick up and k 3 sts from the top of thumb hole, and pick up 1 st on the other side of the hole in the right color to fit the pattern. Total 24 sts.

K straight up in pattern 1¾ inches, then dec: K 2 together at each end of each needle until only 8 sts remain, keeping pattern until the last round. Draw these sts up on the tail of 1 strand and darn smoothly and invisibly back and forth over the tip.

Work all ends into the back of the fabric.

Lighter Checkerboard Mitten

Materials: 1 to 2 ounces light and 2 to 3 ounces dark worsted weight yarn, depending on size.

Equipment: 1 set no. 2 dp knitting needles for ribbing; 1 set no. 5 dp knitting needles, or size needed to knit gauge. Yarn needle for finishing.

Gauge: 7 sts = 1 inch in pattern.

Sizes: Child's 2 to 4 (child's 4 to 6, child's 8 to 10, women's small, women's medium, men's medium, men's large).

Pattern: A multiple of 4 sts and 4 rounds. This pattern can be knit flat if desired, but an extra st should be added at each end for the seam.

First round: K 2 dk, k 2 lt.

Second round: Same as first.

Third round: K 2 lt, k 2 dk.

Fourth round: Same as third.

Note: See General Instructions for Double-knitting before attempting this.

Cuff: Using single strand of dk yarn, cast on 36 (40, 44, 48, 52, 56, 60) sts, dividing these equally on 3 no. 2 dp knitting needles.

K 3, p 1 for 2¼ (2½, 2½, 2¾, 3, 3, 3) inches, striping, if desired, with lt yarn.

Change to no. 5 needles and k 1 round in dk.

Start pattern and thumb gore: For left mitten start thumb gore over the second k rib before the end of round; for right mitten, start above the second rib after the beginning of round.

K in pattern approaching this rib. Then, k both colors, first dk then lt, into what should be the second dk st of a check. Repeat in the next st but lt then dk; repeat in the third st but dk then lt; repeat in the fourth st, lt then dk. You should have 8 sts in the correct pattern sequence, replacing 4.

Inc in the same way again every fourth round above the center of the first inc 3 (3, 4, 4, 5, 5, 6) times for a total of 12 (12, 16, 16, 20, 20, 24) inc sts. K up in pattern without increasing 0 (0, ¾, ¾, ¾, ⅝, 0) inches.

Put 11 (11, 15, 15, 19, 19, 23) thumb gore sts on a string. Cast on 7 over the gap, maintaining correct sequence of colors. Pattern should meet correctly on the far side of the gap.

Hand: K straight up in pattern 2¼ (3, 3¾, 4, 4¼, 4½, 5) inches.

Dec: K 2 together twice at both ends of each needle, every round, maintaining the pattern. You are decreasing 12 every round. The end comes quickly.

When only 10 to 12 sts remain, break yarn, draw the dk tail through the remaining sts, using a yarn needle, and pull up sts firmly. Darn the dk tail back and forth across the tip, smoothly and invisibly.

Thumb: Pick up 1 st from inside of thumb hole in proper color for pattern; pick up 11 (11, 15, 15, 19, 19, 23) sts from string, knitting in correct color; pick up 1 st from side of thumb hole in correct color; pick up 7 from the top of the thumb hole in correct color. The pattern should continue up from the hand on all sides. Total 20 (20, 24, 24, 28, 28, 32) sts.

K straight up in pattern 1½ (1¾, 2¼, 2¼, 2½, 2½, 2¾) inches, then dec quickly, knitting 2 together around until about 8 sts remain. Break yarn, draw remaining sts up firmly on the dk tail, and darn end back and forth invisibly and smoothly over the tip.

Work all tails into the back of the fabric.

Checkerboard Cap

Materials: 2 to 3 ounces dk and 1 to 2 ounces lt worsted weight wool yarn.

Equipment: 1 set 10-inch no. 4 dp (or straight if knitting flat) knitting needles for ribbing. 1 set 10-inch no. 6 dp (or straight) knitting needles, or size needed to knit pattern in correct gauge. Yarn needle for finishing.

Gauge: 6 sts = 1 inch in pattern.

Sizes: Child's small (child's medium, adult medium, adult large), corresponding to a finished cap measuring 16 (18, 20, 22) inches around. For a comfortable fit, a cap should be 2 to 4 inches smaller than the head circumference.

Pattern: See Checkerboard Mitten instructions for pattern and pattern notes.

If knitting flat, purl every other row and read pattern from right to left on purl rows. Add 1 more st to each end for the seam.

Read General Instructions for Double-knitting before starting this project.

Cuff: On no. 4 knitting needles, cast on 96 (108, 120, 132) sts in dk. P 1, k 1 for 2¾ (3½, 4, 4) inches.

Change to no. 6 needles. K 1 round in dk. Start pattern. K straight up in pattern 3¾ (4½, 5, 5) inches.

Adjust sts on needles so that each needle begins with 2 dk sts and ends with 2 lt sts, and there are an equal number of sts on each needle.

Begin dec on first pattern round.

Dec round: K first 2 sts together lt; k second 2 sts together lt. K to 4 sts before end of needle. K next 2 sts together in dk; repeat in next 2 sts. Repeat this dec on the next 2 needles. Total dec 12 sts. The colors may be reversed in some dec rounds.

K 2 (2, 3, 3) rounds, in pattern.

Repeat dec round.

K 1 (1, 2, 2) rounds.

Repeat dec round.

K 0 (0, 1, 1) round.

Now repeat the dec round every round until only 20 sts remain.

Break yarn and pull up remaining sts firmly on both strands, using a yarn needle. Thread the tail through these sts once more, then darn each strand individually into the back of the tip. Work all other loose ends into the back of the fabric.

Attach a pompom to the tip, if you want to.

The cuff should be turned up about half its length so that it also forms the inside band for the cap.

Part Three

Baby Foxes and Goslings
Double-knits for Babies and Small Children

Here are some of the same traditional patterns, knit with a gentler yarn for babies and children up to four years old. The two layers of yarn provided by the pattern and the tightness of the knit make a very warm but light garment in the true Maine tradition.

For babies, these patterns can be knit with synthetic yarn if desired, as it's unlikely that small babies will spend much time in wet snow or fishing on icy waters.

The first patterns are knit on little wee needles — no. 0 and no. 2 — using baby fingering yarn. The second group uses sport-weight yarn and nos. 1, 2, and 4 needles and will be more quickly made.

The sizes overlap the sizes of the worsted weight mittens at size 2 to 4. The worsted weight is more quickly knit and heavier, but is also bulkier — like new denim blue-jeans in babies' sizes. Take your pick.

Baby's Thumbless Mittens

Materials: ½ ounce each light and dark baby yarn or other fingering yarn.

Equipment: 1 set no. 2 dp knitting needles or size needed to obtain correct gauge. 1 set no. 0 dp knitting needles for ribbing. Small yarn needle for finishing.

Gauge: 9½ sts = 1 inch.

Sizes: Newborn. Instructions for 6 months and 1 year are in parentheses.

Patterns: These mittens can be knit in Spruce, Salt and Pepper, Stripes, Checkerboard, or Sawtooth without altering the instructions. Check your gauge carefully (preferably in the yarn store before buying needles) before starting, and study the pattern and pattern notes in the appropriate adult mitten section.

Cuff: With lt yarn and no. 0 dp needles, cast on 44 (48, 56) sts. K 2, p 2 for 2 inches.

Change to no. 2 needles. K 1 round lt.

Start pattern. K straight up in pattern 2¼ (2½, 2¾) inches.

Dec: In the next round, k 2 together 4 times each side. This will absorb 2 patterns. K 2 more rounds.

In next round, k 2 together 4 times each side.

K 1 more round.

Continue to dec every other round until 16 sts remain. Break yarn, draw remaining sts up on the lt strand. Darn this smoothly and invisibly back and forth over tip. Work other tails into fabric.

Ties for mittens: Using no. 2 crochet hook and lt yarn doubled, make a chain 12 inches long for each mitten. Knot one end and string the other in and out through the ribbing, where it joins the stockinette st.

Baby's Helmet

Materials: About 1½ ounce each light and dark baby yarn or other fingering.

Equipment: 1 set no. 2 dp needles, or size needed to obtain correct gauge. No. 2 crochet hook, 2 markers, and small yarn needle for finishing.

Gauge: 10 sts = 1 inch.

Sizes: Newborn. Instructions for 6 months to 1½-year are given in parentheses.

Pattern: Spruce. Check Spruce Mitten Instructions for pattern and pattern notes, and read General Instructions for Double-knitting before starting.

Note: This cap can also be knit in other patterns—Sawtooth, Striped, Checkerboard, or Salt and Pepper. Figure out the decrease based on the adult cap in that pattern. Because the sts in this cap are so tiny and there are so many of them, this is not recommended as a first double-knitting project. Try the patterned cap in this section or some mittens first.

Ear tabs (make 2): Using two no. 2 dp needles, cast on 5(5) sts in lt yarn. K back and forth in stockinette st. Inc 1 st each side every row twice.

Right ear tab only: When there are four rows and 9 sts, make a buttonhole: K 2, k 2 together, loop yarn as if to k, k 2 together, k 3. Next row: P 3, inc one in next st, p loop as a st, complete row.

Start pattern immediately on left ear tab and after buttonhole on right ear tab: K 1 dk, k 3 lt, k 1 dk, k 3 lt, k 1 dk. Second row: P 2 dk, p 1 lt, p 3 dk, p 1 lt, p 2 dk. Catch up the lt strand loosely at each end to even up the tension.

K in pattern 1¾(2) inches. Begin to inc 1 st at each edge every 2 rows, maintaining pattern. When there are 37(43) sts, put aside and make the second ear tab.

Now, using 4 needles, pick up and k all 37(43) sts from left ear tab; in correct color, cast on 43(49) sts for front; pick up all 37(43) sts for the right ear tab, and in correct colors, cast on 23(25) sts for the back. Total 140(160) sts. Adjust 1 to 2 sts, if necessary, to make pattern meet at the edges of the ear tabs.

K straight up 2⅝ inches in pattern. End with second pattern around (3 lt, 1 dk).

Now, adjust sts so that one needle has all 43(49) front sts. Put markers above the 2 back edges of the ear tabs, and be sure there's a lt center st beginning each needle and just after each marker. Dec at markers and edges of front "panel."

Dec: *K first 2 sts together dk; k second 2 sts together dk. K in pattern to last 4 sts before next dec point. K next 2 sts together lt, last 2 sts together dk.* Repeat ** between markers around.

Dec this way every sixth round twice, every fourth round twice, every second round once, then every round until 36 to 40 sts remain.

Break yarn, thread the lt tail through the remaining sts and draw up firmly. Darn this tail smoothly and invisibly back and forth across the tip. Work all other tails into the back of fabric.

Single crochet around whole edge twice, pulling up the edge on inside curves and allowing extra sts on outside curves. Sew a small button on the left ear tab.

Total circumference at brim edge 140(160) sts or 14(16) inches. Total height from tab end to crown: 9.6(11) inches.

Baby Foxes and Goslings Mittens with Thumbs

Materials: About ¾ ounce dk and ½ ounce lt colored sports weight yarn, preferably wool.

Equipment: 1 set no. 2 dp knitting needles, or size needed to knit gauge. 1 set no. 1 dp knitting needles for ribbing. Yarn needle for finishing.

Gauge: 9 sts = 1 inch.

Sizes: Instructions are for size 6 months to 1 year. Instructions for size 2 to 3 years and 4 years are in parentheses.

Pattern: Fox and Geese is a multiple of 6 sts and 6 rounds; incs and decs are made almost only in the first round. These mittens are knit without a third color for the horizontal lines.

For clarity, 1 band means all 6 rounds; 1 block means all 6 sts in one round.

First round: k 1 dk, k 3 lt, d 2 dk around.

Second round: k 1 lt, k 1 dk around.

Third round: k 2 lt, k 1 dk around.

Fourth round: k 1 lt, k 1 dk around.

Fifth round: k 1 dk, k 3 lt, k 2 dk around.

Sixth round: k dk around.

This pattern can't be knit flat. Be sure to read General Instructions for Double-knitting before starting.

Cuff: Cast on 40 (48, 52) sts in dk yarn with no. 1 needles. K 2, p 2 for 1¼ (1½, 1¾) inches.

Change to no. 2 needles. K 1 round in dk, increasing 2 (0, 2).

Start pattern: K top half (whole, whole) band of pattern.

Thumb gore: At beginning of next band of pattern, inc 6 sts: For left mitten, k to second vertical before beginning of round. For right mitten, k to second vertical after beginning of round. K 1 dk (vertical), k both colors, dk then lt, into next st without twisting or knitting into the back side of the st. Wrap lt yarn on right needle as if to k. K both colors into the next st, lt then dk. Wrap dk yarn as if to k. K both colors into the next st, dk then lt. Wrap lt yarn as if to k, then k next st lt as usual. Total inc is 6 sts. This is the only inc in these mittens.

Complete band.

Take off thumb: On the dk round (pattern round 6) and before knitting them, take off 11 thumb gore sts, leaving a dk vertical on both sides. Put these sts on a string. Cast on 5 over the gap in dk and continue around.

K straight up in pattern until 2¾ (3¼, 3¾) inches from top of cuff.

Dec for 6 months to 1 year: On pattern round 5, k 2 dk together, k 1 lt, k 2 together lt, k 1 dk and repeat around. Next round, k 1, k 2 together in dk around. Next round, k 2 together dk, k 1 lt, k 2 together lt, repeat around.

Dec for size 2 to 3: Start dec at sixth pattern round of the fifth band of pattern: K 1 dk, k 2 together dk, repeat around. Next round k 2 together dk, k 1 lt, k 2 together lt, k 1 dk; repeat around. Next round, k 2 together around, using the opposite alternation of color from the preceding round.

Dec for size 4: Start dec at third pattern round of the sixth band of pattern. K 1 dk, *k 2 together lt, k 1 dk.* Repeat from * to * around. Next round, k 1 dk, k 2 together lt, repeat around. Next round, k 1 lt, k 2 together dk and repeat around.

Keep decreasing until 8 to 12 sts remain. Break yarn, pull sts up on the tail of one strand, using yarn needle. Darn tail smoothly and invisibly back and forth over tip.

Thumb: Pick up and k 1 st from palm side of thumb hole in dk, pick up and k dk 11 sts from string, pick up and k 1 st dk from back side of thumb hole, pick up and k, in correct color sequence, 5 sts from top of thumb hole.

K straight up in pattern, taking care not to pull yarn too tight on 3 dk-3 lt rounds, for ¾ (1, 1¼) inch.

Dec sharply: First round, k 1, k 2 together around; second round, k 2 together around until 6 to 8 sts remain. Break yarn, draw sts up firmly on tail of one strand. Darn this smoothly and invisibly back and forth over the tip of the thumb to reinforce it. Work all other tails into the back of the fabric.

Checkerboard Mittens

Materials: About ½ ounce lt-and ¾ ounce dk- colored sports weight yarn, preferably wool.

Equipment: 1 set no. 1 dp knitting needles for ribbing. 1 set no. 3 dp needles, or size needed to knit correct gauge.

Gauge: 9 sts = 1 inch in pattern.

Sizes: Instructions are for size 6 months to 1 year. Instructions for sizes 2, 3, and 4 years are in parentheses.

Pattern: Checkerboard is based on a multiple of 4 sts and 4 rounds. It can be knit flat; an extra st should be added to each end for the seam.

First pattern round: K 2 dk, k 2 lt.

Second pattern round: Same as first.

Third pattern round: K 2 lt, k 2 dk.

Fourth pattern round: Same as third.

Note: Read General Instruction for Double-knitting before starting.

Cuff: Cast on 44 (48, 52, 56) sts in dk yarn with no. 1 dp knitting needles. K 2, p 2 for 1½ (1¾, 2, 2¼) inches.

Change to no. 3 needles. K 1 round in dk.

Start pattern. K 2 rounds of pattern.

Begin thumb gore: At beginning of third round, inc 4 sts: In the second dk st of a pair, k both colors into the st, first dk then lt. Repeat in next st, but first lt then dk; in the third st, dk then lt; in the fourth st, lt then dk. K the next st dk and continue pattern around.

K 3 more rounds in pattern, then inc 4 sts again, the same way, directly above the center of the first inc (which will look slightly like the trademark on the Heinz's Ketchup bottle). The colors will be reversed this time. K 3 more rounds in pattern, then inc 4 sts again, the same way, directly above the center of the other 2 incs. Total inc 12 sts.

K straight up in pattern 2 more rounds.

Take 15 thumb gore sts off and put them on a string. Cast on 3 (3, 7, 7) sts over the gap. K straight up in pattern until 2¾ (3¼, 3¾, 4½) inches above top of cuff.

Dec: K 2 together twice at the beginning and end of each needle. Keep the pattern by continuing the 2/2 sequence until the last 2 rounds. When there are only 8 to 12 sts left, break yarn and, after threading tail through the remaining sts, draw them up firmly. Darn the tail back and forth across the tip.

Thumb: Pick up and k 15 sts from the thumb gore, 1 from each side of the thumb hole, and 3 (3, 7, 7) from the top of the thumb hole, knitting in correct color for pattern.

K straight up in pattern for ¾ (1, 1¼, 1½) inches.

Dec sharply: K 2 together around until 6 to 8 sts remain. Break yarn, draw remaining sts up on the dk tail, then darn this tail back and forth invisibly over the tip.

Work all loose ends into the back of the fabric.

Sawtooth Mittens

Because of the 2 pattern rounds knit in a single color, and because the design doesn't pull up the fabric, this pattern makes a much lighter mitten than Checkerboard, although not as light as a single-knit mitten.

Materials: ½ ounce each mc (main color) and cc (contrasting color) sports weight yarn.

Equipment: 1 set no. 1 dp knitting needles for ribbing. 1 set no. 2 dp knitting needles or size required to knit gauge. Yarn needle for finishing.

Gauge: 9 sts = 1 inch in pattern.

Sizes: Instructions are for newborn to 6 months. Instructions for sizes 2, 3, and 4 are in parentheses.

Pattern: Sawtooth is a multiple of 4 sts and 5 rounds. This can be knit flat only with dp needles.

The pattern can be reversed for the left mitten, so the sawteeth point in the opposite direction. This pattern is for the right mitten.

First round: K cc around.

Second round: K 1 mc, k 3 cc, around.

Third round: K 2 mc, k 2 cc, around.

Fourth round: K 3 mc, k 1 cc, around.

Fifth round: K mc around.

Please read General Instructions for Double-knitting before starting.

Cuff: Cast on in mc 40 (48, 52, 56) sts on 3 no. 1 dp needles. K 2, p 2 for 1½ (1¾, 2, 2¼) inches.

Change to no. 2 needles. K 1 round in mc. Start pattern.

At beginning of the second round of pattern (k 1 mc, k 3 cc), inc 4 sts: k both colors into the first st, first mc then cc; between sts loop the cc yarn as if to k; k both colors, cc then mc, into the next st; loop cc yarn as if to k; k next st cc as usual and continue around in pattern.

Inc the same way in the second pattern round of the next 2 bands of pattern. Total inc 12 sts. Complete the last band of pattern. K 1 band of pattern without increasing at all for the 2 larger sizes.

On first pattern round, without knitting them, take off 15 thumb-gore sts and put them on a string or safety pin. Cast on 3 (3, 7, 7) sts over the gap in cc and continue around.

K straight up in pattern until 2¾ (3¼, 3¾, 4½) inches above top of cuff.

Dec: K first pattern round. Second pattern round, k 1 mc, k 1 cc, k 2 together cc; repeat around. Third round, k 2 mc, k 1 cc around. Fourth round, k 2 together around in mc. Fifth round, k 2 together in cc, continuing until 10 to 12 sts remain.

Break yarn, thread cc tail through remaining sts, using yarn needle; pull up firmly and darn this tail smoothly and invisibly across the tip.

Put the 15 thumb gore sts onto 2 needles, without knitting them. Pick up one st from the side of the thumb hole and k in mc. Pick up and k 3 (3, 7, 7) sts in mc from top of thumb hole. Pick up and k 1 st in mc from other side of thumb hole. K around in cc (first pattern round). Total 20 (20, 24, 24) sts. The pattern will be upside down on the inside of the thumb from the pattern just above it on the palm. Don't panic.

K straight up in pattern ¾ (1, 1¼, 1½) inch.

Dec sharply: First round, k 1, k 2 together, sticking

somewhat to pattern; second round, k 2 together, alternating colors if it fits the pattern. Break yarn, thread 1 tail through remaining sts, using yarn needle, and pull up firmly. Darn invisibly and smoothly back and forth over the tip. Work all loose ends into the back of fabric.

Reverse the direction of the sawteeth, if you want to, for the left mitten. Start the thumb gore in the last 5 sts of the second pattern round.

Patterned Cap

This cap can be made in the Fox and Geese pattern or any of the other double-knit patterns in this section.

Materials: About 1½ ounce dk and ¾ ounce lt sports weight yarn. One ⅜-inch button.

Equipment: 1 set no. 2 dp knitting needles for ribbing. For Fox and Geese, Salt and Pepper, and Sawtooth: 1 set no. 4 knitting needles, or size needed to knit correct gauge. For Stripes, Spruce, or Checkerboard: 1 set no. 5 knitting needles or size needed to knit correct gauge.

Gauge: 8½ sts = 1 inch in pattern.

Sizes: Newborn to 6 months (6 months to 1½ year, 2 to 4 years old). This corresponds to a finished hat circumference of 14 (16, 18) inches.

Pattern: See the mitten instructions for the pattern you wish to use and read the accompanying pattern notes. For Sawtooth, use the pattern under Child's Sawtooth Mittens.

Be sure to read General Instructions for Double-knitting, if you haven't already, before starting.

This cap is knit from the top down.

Cast on 15 (17, 20) sts in dk yarn, evenly divided among 3 no. 2 dp knitting needles. In the next round, inc 1 in every st. Total 30 (34, 40) sts.

Then rib: K 1, p 1 around. Rib 3 rounds.

In next round, inc in every st. Total 60 (68, 80) sts.

Then rib 5 rounds, k 1, p 1.

In the next round, inc in every st until there are 120 (136, 156) sts. For any pattern based on a multiple of 6 sts, add 2 more in the next round for the second size only.

Rib 2 more rounds, k 1, p 1, then change to no. 4 (or 5) needles.

K 1 round in dk (or for Fox and Geese, red).

Start pattern: K in pattern for 2⅝ (3, 3½) inches, or as near as possible. Do complete the pattern. Finish with 1 round of dk (or for Fox and Geese, red).

Change to no. 2 needles and k 1, p 1 for 6 rounds.

Bind off: Bind off 17 (19, 22) sts at beginning of round for back of cap. K 1, p 1 across 34 (39, 45) sts for ear tab. Bind off 35 (39, 44) sts for front of cap. K 1, p 1 across 34 (39, 45) sts for second ear tab. For Fox and Geese, add 1 more st to each ear tab in second size only.

On one ear tab, continue k 1, p 1, ribbing back and forth, decreasing 1 st at the end of every row until the tab is 2 (2¼, 2½) inches below the edge of the cuff. Then dec 1 st both ends every row until 8 (10, 10) sts remain. Continue to rib back and forth for 1½ (1¾, 2) more inches. Bind off.

Repeat on the other ear tab.

For boy's cap, using tail of knitting, crochet a button-loop on the end of the left ear tab. For girl's cap, crochet a buttonloop on the end of the right ear tab, using the tail from knitting. For both, continue to single crochet all the way around the edge of the cap until you reach the buttonloop again. Single crochet around this too, making it stronger, then tie off just beyond it.

Work all loose ends into the back of the fabric. Using the tail from casting on and a yarn needle, catch up all the cast-on sts and draw them up firmly, so there's no hole in the top of the cap. Darn invisibly and smoothly back and forth over the tip.

Acknowledgments

This book was not entirely my creation. It depends heavily on all the women who still knit these mittens or remember their mothers or grandmothers knitting them, and on women and organizations who have collected and promoted the patterns in Maine and Canada.

Without Nora Johnson of Five Islands, the book would not have been possible. Mrs. Johnson remembered with great precision three patterns and the mitten instructions that go with them. A perfectionist as a knitter (although not an unpleasant one), she strives to make every line of the mitten emphasize the lines of the hand, and to choose striking color combinations in an older tradition than today's heathers and naturals.

Mrs. Johnson showed me how to make Striped, Salt and Pepper, and Fox and Geese mittens and helped me learn several different tricks of Maine knitting. She painstakingly went over my instructions, finding several outright errors and helping me to clarify the directions. Many, many thanks!

I am indebted to Pat Zamore of Yankee Yarns in Brunswick for introducing me to Mrs. Johnson, for putting me on the double-knit mitten trail, and for information on Fleece-stuffed mittens in Maine. She also gave much technical assistance.

Judy McGrath, a crafts researcher for *Them Days* magazine, and Peggy Lough, both of Happy Valley, Labrador, helped me with instructions for Fleece-stuffed Mittens and with the Labrador mitten-knitting scene. Laura Jackson of Happy Valley showed me more Labrador "mitts" and introduced me to local knitters.

Joan Waldron of the Nova Scotia Museum in Halifax put me in contact with craftspeople in Nova Scotia, Newfoundland and Labrador. By her great enthusiasm she has helped promote the old tradition of double-knitting mittens in Nova Scotia. She also lent me a complete collection of Nova Scotia graphed patterns with matching swatches of knit.

Janetta Dexter of Hampden, Nova Scotia, who collected and published a group of Nova Scotian double-knit patterns, helped me to name and trace several patterns held in common between Maine and Nova Scotia. She is also largely responsible for reviving the craft in her province.

Laura Ridgewell of West Point gave me the idea for this book when she asked me to find her a fishermen's wet mitten pattern. The search led to many other ideas and connections.

Jackie Trask, Diane Calder, and Elizabeth Bergh, all of Chebeague Island, and Marge Creaser of Boothbay Harbor provided much of the information on wet mittens. The instructions were written by Elizabeth Bergh, based on a pair of mittens knit by Jackie Trask's late grandmother, Minnie Doughty.

Mrs. Carr, whom I know by no other name, of Bartlettyarns at Harmony, kindly provided me with instructions — which I changed somewhat — for Fox and Geese shooting gloves and Spruce mittens.

My husband, Erik, a naval architect, deserves piles of thanks for showing me how to compute knitting patterns and how to draft cap sizes. He also took many of the photographs shown in this book and accompanied me on a two-week mitten tour of the Maritime Provinces.

Thanks also to the Nova Scotia Museum for letting me use their photo of nippers and the accompanying information.